Top
Table Te

Top-class Table Tennis

Jill Hammersley MBE
and Donald Parker

EP Publishing Limited

Copyright © 1983 Jill Hammersley and Donald Parker

ISBN 0 7158 0817 6 (casebound)
ISBN 0 7158 0831 1 (paperback)

First edition 1983
Published by EP Publishing Limited, Bradford Road,
East Ardsley, Wakefield, West Yorkshire, WF3 2JN, England

British Library Cataloguing in Publication Data

Hammersley, Jill
   Top-class table tennis.
   1. Table tennis
   I. Title   II. Parker, Donald
   796.34'6   GV1005

   ISBN 0-7158-0817-6
   ISBN 0-7158-0831-1 pbk

Design: Douglas Martin Associates
Illustrations: Stephen Beaumont
Typeset in 10½/13½ pt Paladium by PFB Art & Type Limited, Leeds, England.
Printed and bound in Italy by Legatoria Editoriale Giovanni Olivotto, Vicenza.

This book is copyright under the Berne Convention. All rights are reserved.
Apart from any fair dealing for the purposes of private study, research,
criticism or review, as permitted under the Copyright Act, 1956, no part of this
publication may be reproduced, stored in a retrieval system, or transmitted in
any form or by any means, electronic, electrical, chemical, mechanical, optical,
photocopying, recording or otherwise, without the prior permission of the
copyright owner. Enquiries should be addressed to the publishers.

Contents

About the authors, 7

1 Introduction, 10

2 The right equipment for you, 13

3 Getting to grips with the basics, 18

4 Advanced techniques, 36

5 Service and receive, 67

6 Footwork, 85

7 Successful doubles play, 93

8 Healthy body, healthy game, 101

9 The role of the coach, 107

10 Combination bat – myth or magic? 111

11 Ball in the mind? 123
Table tennis psychology – the right mental approach

12 Winning tactics, 135

13 Training through the seasons, 147
Periodisation

14 The Chinese scene, 157

15 What now for table tennis? 171

This book is dedicated to Dave and Jan, without whom writing it would have been impossible.

We would also like to thank Butterfly (UK) Ltd for the use of equipment, and the Chinese photographers who generously gave us the photographs reproduced in chapter 14. Other photographic credits are as follows:

Malcolm Anderson: 94(t), 142.

Brian Ashton: 140.

Ian Ball: 46, 56, 59, 63, 66, 68, 81, 83, 87, 88, 93, 96, 98(t), 99(b), 100, 112, 127, 141, 156, 158, 172.

Honéczy Barnabás: 44, 51, 69, 71, 73, 86, 91, 98(b), 99(t), 109, 110, 117—120, 134, 139.

Steve Hilton: 115.

Šín Josef: 130.

Gerard C. Kellett: 7, 19, 20, 24—33, 38—42, 47—49, 53—55, 57, 58, 60—62, 74—77, 103, 105.

Jiří Pekárek: 146.

Slough Observer: 34.

About the authors

Born in Carshalton, Surrey, Jill Hammersley was introduced to table tennis at the tender age of ten years by her elder brother Paul.

He had been playing for some time when he was persuaded one Saturday afternoon by their parents to take his sister along for a knockabout in the unlikely surroundings of the Slough British Legion Club. Practices were held there every Saturday, Tuesday and Thursday nights. Clearly hooked by her first visit, Jill was never to miss another session.

To the surprise of some of the older members she showed the sort of resilience not normally found in one so young, with a sound temperament and dogged refusal to part with points without a fight.

It was only a matter of time before she was to win her first title, the under-eleven event of the Crescent Girls Open at nearby Sittingbourne. It was to be the first in a long line of successes in a career that has spanned over fifteen years and that culminated in her toppling the legendary Maria Alexandru of Romania to take the coveted European Ladies Singles title at Prague in 1976.

At fifteen she made her national debut for the junior England team against Holland. A full England cap was to follow shortly after, and heralded an international success story which has so far included over four hundred appearances for her country, more than anyone else in the history of the game.

At sixteen, with a bright career in the game beckoning, she forsook any thoughts of academic success and left school. Her first job took the form of a contract with a firm of sports goods manufacturers. Between training camps, tournaments and international commitments, what little time was left was spent in the office at Putney, sticking transfers onto tennis rackets and typing the odd invoice.

In 1969, thanks to a cheap flight (available through her father, who worked for British Airways) and a modest allowance from her sponsor, she packed her bags for a month's training in Nagoya, Japan, then the mecca of the modern game. She returned equipped with a new and tenacious approach that was quickly to take her to the number one spot in the English

An interesting double exposure of the author.

women's rankings, and that gave her a defence which few of her European contemporaries could penetrate.

In 1971, as part of the English squad, she toured the People's Republic of China, one of the first of a handful of Western visitors to enter that country since its Cultural Revolution.

The 1970s produced a string of successes too numerous to mention. Most notably, these included being three times winner of the Ladies Singles title at the Commonwealth Championships, the English Open and the Hungarian Open. Even in the 1980s there has been no let up in the consistently high standard of performance she has set herself. Having appeared on over seventy occasions in European League fixtures she boasts a success rate of over seventy-five percent. Her skill as a tactician has not been confined to singles events. In 1976, at Prague, she partnered Linda Jarvis to win the European Women's Doubles title.

In 1979 she made the journey to Buckingham Palace to receive the MBE, the first table-tennis player to receive such an award since the heady days of Johnny Leach.

Early in 1982 she was appointed Captain of the English Junior Girls team, bringing her enormous experience to bear on the development of a very young side. Later that year she married co-author Donald Parker, National Coach, English Junior Captain and former English Women's Captain.

Donald learnt his table tennis at a young age, in the holiday camps of Sir Billy Butlin and at home in the rather cramped conditions of the garage, where his father Jim had installed a home-made table.

At only eight years old, he made his local league debut for Preston's Deepdale Club. At thirteen he represented the Lancashire Juniors, and in 1973, at fifteen, he played for England in the European Youth Championships.

He finished his junior career ranked number two in Great Britain, being narrowly displaced from the number-one spot by Desmond Douglas. Unlike many of his contemporaries, he successfully made the transition from junior to senior level, gaining his first senior cap against Hungary at Crawley in 1973. He has been in the top ten of the national rankings ever since.

More significant, though, has been Donald's impact on the coaching scene. Leaving Hutton Grammar School (near Preston) in 1974, he went on to Loughborough University to study Physical Education and Biology. On graduating four years later with an honours degree, he was quickly snapped up by the English Table Tennis Association and appointed National Coach for the North of England.

At only twenty-two years old he found himself in charge of the development of an expanding coaching programme and managing the region's 'centre of excellence'. This was in addition to his responsibility for the English junior sides, and captaining of the English ladies side, led by his wife-to-be Jill.

Since his involvement, all these areas have gone from strength to strength. The English Boys Cadet side were European Champions at Topolcany, Czechoslovakia, in 1982 — which can only bode well for England's future.

His talents as a strategist, coach and captain have not been restricted to helping younger players. In 1982 he also took a relatively inexperienced men's side to the Commonwealth Championships in Bombay and returned with a gold medal in the team event.

Despite a hectic lifestyle, which can often take them to the four corners of the globe, Jill and Don have still found the time to run summer schools for people of all ages, abilities and nationalities at their home in the beautiful village of Dolphinholme, near Lancaster.

Both share an infectious enthusiasm and insatiable appetite for the game, through which they will doubtless remain a strong influence on the direction of English table tennis for years to come.

1 Introduction

You would be forgiven for thinking that table tennis is a simple game — a table, two bats, a ball — what could be simpler than that? But anyone playing nowadays, even at the lowest local league level, would be forced to disagree.

No other racket sport has changed quite so much as table tennis. In writing this book I have been very aware of the game's chameleon nature that has gradually caused it to develop into a science. Tacticians, mathematicians, physicians and magicians — all these strange beings now dwell on its periphery. Perhaps it would be very refreshing to sweep aside such high-flown approaches in favour of more old-fashioned qualities such as dedication, application and talent. But while the latter are of course still essential, to do such a thing would be to mislead you.

Irrespective of the level at which you may be involved, be it player, coach, parent or even spectator, it would be foolish to ignore the fact that table tennis is now a fast and complex sport. Thankfully, the phrase 'ping pong' is virtually extinct.

Not everybody is able to play for their country, and I have been one of the lucky few in this respect. However, I firmly believe that most people playing table tennis today are quite capable of improving their game with relatively little effort. I have written this book with this theme throughout — that of trying to help raise the standard of play. In particular I have tried to pitch most of my advice at the grass-roots level. Were it not for the enthusiasm and contribution of the local league players and hard-working officials, there would not be an English Table Tennis Association; and this applies equally to the dedication of players and officials in other countries. In this sense I owe many unknown people a lot for the living they have given me. I hope that sharing the knowledge and experience I have gained over the years will go some way toward repaying this debt.

Though table tennis is no longer an amusing hobby or pastime played by gentlefolk on the parlour table, there is no single scientific secret for instant success. If there were, you could safely bet that I would have included it in these pages! Success has a lot to do with a hunger and a deep-rooted, burning will to win. If you are hungry enough for victory, you will reach your full potential.

One of the most immediately visible changes in today's game is the bats players now use. I could not begin to work through the hundreds of varieties and combinations that arrive daily on the market. What I have tried to do is to offer some guidance on how to make the most appropriate choice for your particular style and level of play. From there it is a personal choice as to what suits *you* best and gives *you* the most favourable results.

This same maxim also applies to stroke play. I have examined the four basic strokes and looked in some detail at the many advanced techniques now practised in the international game. At the end of the day you must decide on your own version. Who knows, in years to come, when another table-tennis book is written, you may be the writer's inspiration for the model way in which to tackle a forehand drive. As I said before, the game is continually changing and it is those who respond to change, who adapt and become the innovators, that reap the rewards.

A crucial impact in recent years has been the development of the areas of service and receive. Whereas at one time they were just a means of starting a rally, now they can quite easily be the deciding factor between winner and loser. The key innovators here have been the Chinese, and I have taken the opportunity to examine these developments.

It also goes without saying these days that to enjoy any game fully you need to be fit. In close consultation with my co-author and husband, Don Parker, I have attempted to provide the player of today with a few tips on the specific type of training needed. Also we have looked at how to integrate this into planning your preparation for the season.

It is often said that there is a fun element lacking in the modern game that was more prominent in its earlier days. In some ways I have to agree, and I think that this is perhaps typified by the way the doubles game has been neglected. If played to a tactical pattern it can be a rewarding change from the more favoured singles game. More importantly, it can sometimes tip the balance in team matches. Chapter 7, 'Successful doubles play', looks at different strategies with direct reference to many of the game's leading players.

In preparing this book, I have talked at length to many of the top coaches. In the course of my discussions it occurred to me that these valuable contributors have been sadly overlooked in many table-tennis publications. While this book is largely directed to the player, I have attempted to remedy this defect by trying, wherever possible, to involve the coach. I can personally vouch for the value that good coaching has had in my career. I hope that the chapters dealing with tactics and table-tennis psychology form the basis for fruitful discussion.

1. Introduction

If there is one thing that table tennis is not lacking in, it is controversy. At the time of writing, the game is at something of a watershed in its development. This has been largely brought about by the momentous increase in the use of the combination bat. As an exponent myself, I could hardly ignore its impact, and I have therefore devoted a chapter to an examination of the combination-bat game and the arguments that currently surround it.

The endless discussion of its pros and cons that has followed the combination bat's progress has in turn cast the spotlight on table-tennis officialdom. It is my feeling that they would rather have basked in the shadows and hoped for this insistent pain in the neck to go away. I have, therefore, looked critically at the position of the game's decision-making bodies in relation to our position as players.

I would like to conclude by giving you this quotation from Leslie Woolard, editor of the now defunct *Table Tennis* magazine, which still has a peculiar poignancy today: 'A sport which can develop in such an unprecedented way in such difficult times must have something worthwhile. It has. But it is not something for nothing, for you cannot get more out of a game than you put into it.'

2 The right equipment for you

The bat

At one time, table tennis was a very inexpensive game to play. All you needed was a bat, a shirt and pair of plimsolls. The bats were all the same, basic quality, and the price stayed the same for years. This is because there was very little spin in the game. Ask any veteran player and they will recall with fondness the days of the hard 'Barna' bat, not only from a nostalgic point of view, but also from an economic one!

They have some justification. Choosing a bat these days is mesmerising. There are so many variations, and you can now buy a table-tennis bat which costs more than a high-quality professional tennis racket. Thirty years ago, the best table-tennis bat on the market cost less than a set of new strings for a tennis racket.

In this chapter I will try and help you make the right choice and tell you of some of the pitfalls to watch out for in buying a bat.

The majority of bats on the market nowadays are covered by what is termed 'sponge rubber'. As the diagram shows, this type of surface is composed of, firstly, a layer of sponge rubber (which comes in varying thicknesses) and, secondly, a layer of pimpled rubber. This latter component is stuck onto the sponge, either pimples first (reversed) or pimples outwards; the combined unit of sponge and rubber must not exceed 4 mm.

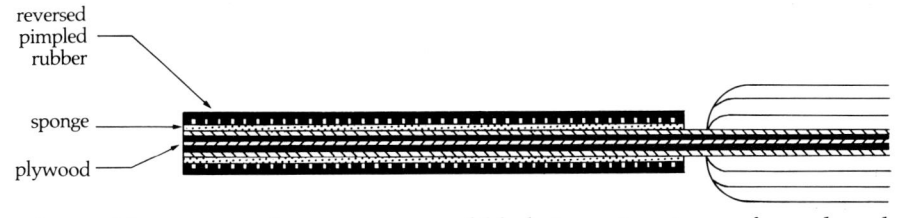

The various layers of a typical sponge bat.

You can now buy an uncovered blade in various types of wood, and loose sheets of whatever kind of rubber suits your style of play. You glue these together yourself. For ease of reference, when I talk about rubber I am in fact referring to the combined unit of sponge and pimpled rubber.

Some reversed rubbers can grip the ball well, and hence are capable of putting a lot of spin on it. Others impart little or no spin at all because they have no grip. The thicker and harder the rubber, the faster it is, but you will not be able to control it as easily. Rubber with the pimples outwards gives little spin, but is good for hitting the ball hard and flat; however, it is not always easy to control. Hard wood will make a faster bat, whereas softer wood helps control. Some players use 'combination bats', which have fast rubber on one side and slow 'negative' rubber on the other: both might be the same colour, and produce the same sound. With all these variables, choosing the right bat has become a science in itself!

For the time being I will leave aside the question of the 'combination bat' and also the pimpled-outward type of rubber; that deserves a chapter to itself!

Probably the best way to choose a bat is to consider the type of player you are and to aim for a bat with the characteristics that will suit your game.

Beginner

BLADE: The first and most important thing to consider is the handle. Choose one that feels comfortable and fits in your hand well. The wood for the blade should be the 'all round' variety, light, not too hard and made up of about five layers (5-ply).

RUBBER: The key factor you want is control, so the rubber you select should be no thicker than 1.5 mm. Spin is not terribly important, nor is speed, so aim for the bottom half of the price bracket. What you are looking for is to be able to feel the ball on the bat as you are playing.

Intermediate

BLADE: Hopefully you have been playing for some time now, and you have mastered the basic shots. Nevertheless, it will do no harm to stick with the same blade for the time being.

RUBBER: Control still remains the most important factor, but you can now consider increasing the speed and spin characteristics of your rubber. However, there is no need to go thicker than 1.5 mm. Depending on the style of play you are adopting, you might want more spin only, but the same speed as before, and there are rubbers available which allow for this.

Inter-league player (attacker)

BLADE: If you are a fast-loop drive player you might look at a harder, heavier bat with more layers in the blade. Try to stick with the same handle, though.

Although they have not been as popular as first anticipated, you might try a carbon-fibre blade. The thin layers of hard carbon fibres in the layers of the blade create the effect of an increased 'sweet spot'.

RUBBER: The all-out topspin attacker needs a thick rubber. If you want more spin as well, then you will have to sacrifice a little speed. This is because the harder, faster rubbers do not allow the ball to remain too long on the bat. A softer rubber will allow that fraction of a second longer for you to spin the ball. Also, it might be worth your while to consider a thinner sponge on one side, perhaps on your backhand where more control might be needed.

After all, it does not matter how fast you are and how much spin you produce, if you cannot keep the ball on the table!

Inter-league player (defensive)

BLADE: Quite obviously, the defensive player will be looking for a softwood, slow blade; this is what I play with. However, you can alter the type of blade to compensate for any shortcomings in the rubber you use. For example, if the rubber is a little too slow you could consider a faster blade. Different blades have far less effect on the ball than the rubber does.

RUBBER: Here you are looking for control and spin, so choose a thin rubber of about 1 mm, but with plenty of adhesive quality.

Alternatively, you might try the combination bat I have already mentioned.

There are a number of excellent mail-order firms which cater for all different styles. Their catalogues go into great detail about the science of bat selection. But remember, the best bat in the world will not make you a great player. Few players are really capable of exploiting the bats and the various rubbers to their full advantage. So there is no need to spend a lot of money, which is a common fault.

Equipment distributors and manufacturers are like any other businessmen — they will respond to trends in the game, and are concerned with selling their own product. Bear this in mind when looking through their lavish catalogues.

A recent trend I have noticed concerns the glue that sticks the rubber to the blade. Some of the fast-looping top European players have taken to varnishing their blades; this makes them harder and thus faster. They then stick the sheets of rubber on with the sort of rubber cement you find in bicycle-tyre repair kits. This adds to the elasticity of the rubber, giving a faster, catapult effect. I would not recommend it. Bats are fast enough as it is, and few people can actually control them except the top players. But I wonder — how long will it be before the manufacturers catch on to this craze?

Hints and tips

Finally, a few hints.

Try and get yourself a spare bat, preferably a replica of the other one, because they are easily lost or broken.

When you are playing in very cold conditions, warm your bat and hand first. This is because the rubber's elastic properties are more pronounced when warmer. Your hand is no good when stiff and cold, either, as you will not be able to control the ball.

There are a lot of rubber cleaners on the market, and most of them are not exactly cheap. I use soap and water, ensuring that it does not come into contact with the sponge part of the rubber. It is quite sufficient, and a lot cheaper. Try and keep the rubber as clean as possible throughout matches or tournaments.

While on the subject of water, remember that sweat on the bat is not only illegal but it means that your bat cannot grip the ball. Watch out for this.

When you stick the rubber on, take care not to cut away the brand name. This is illegal under ITTF regulations, because you must be able to demonstrate to the umpire that you are using a recognisably accepted make.

Playing conditions can affect the ball as much as the bat. Many players believe that a large expansive hall makes it move more slowly, while a smaller room will have the opposite effect. A carpeted floor will supposedly slow the ball down, as well.

Clothing

Table tennis, when played properly, is a physically demanding game. Like any other sport you need the right clothing — stuff that is comfortable and will let you move freely. So jeans are out. Make sure, though, that your playing clothes are dark in colour as the rules of the game stipulate. Tracksuits and sweatshirts are very useful additions to your table-tennis wardrobe. They will keep you warm in cold halls when you are not playing, and will help prevent your muscles from stiffening up.

I feel strongly that table-tennis clothing needs brightening up, and one of the reasons why it is so dull are the constraints placed on it by the laws of the game. For example, I was once involved in a company which was new in this field and manufactured bright new designs. The collar and sleeve trims on my shirt differed in colour slightly from the rest of it. Unfortunately, the rules of the game do not permit this sort of deviation. As a result I was reprimanded by Officialdom, though my opponents openly conceded that they were in no way distracted. What a negative approach at a time when this sport needs every help it can get! Our governing bodies should have a long hard look at the success of other sports — tennis, for example — and then set about reforming their archaic rules about dress.

Footwear

A light pair of sports shoes is needed for table tennis, with a soft rubber sole and good tread. Because your weight is concentrated on the balls of your feet, or towards your instep, be careful to select a shoe that will give support in this area.

I tend to consider my socks as important as my pumps. Because table-tennis shoes need to be light, there is never quite enough cushioning in the insole. So to avoid blisters I wear well-padded socks.

Kitbag

A sports bag is a valuable asset in this game. More important, though, is what you carry around in it. Mine contains the following:
- A plastic bottle full of a glucose-based drink.
- My spare bats.
- A towel.
- A first-aid kit — mostly sticking plasters to stop blistering.
- A stopwatch. I like to know how long a game has been running, because my defensive style of play often gets me involved in expedite games.
- The notebook in which I record many of my matches.

Table tennis need not be an expensive game to play if you choose the right equipment. Hopefully, you can now go shopping and still come back with change to start saving for your own table as well!

3 Getting to grips with the basics

When we use a term like 'basic', there is always a danger that it will be interpreted as somehow meaning 'simple' or 'easy'. Let me assure you, where table tennis is concerned nothing could be further from the truth.

Indeed, it is often useful even for players who think themselves competent and experienced to reconsider their approach to this fundamental aspect of the game. As in the parable, the man who builds his house on rock will be much more secure than the man who builds his house on sand. The same goes for table tennis. The player who takes time now to master the basic strokes will find that it pays him untold dividends later, when others will be trying to run before they can walk. I realise this may sound old-fashioned, but experience has shown me how true it is. It is no good being able to play a superb forehand topspin if you only get one out of five on the table, or if you cannot play a relatively simple backhand push when the occasion demands it.

On the sporting front, we English are a nation of imitators, tending to copy advanced techniques too early in an attempt to emulate the stars. Youngsters in particular are obsessed with looking impressive, and it is this sort of vanity which often proves their undoing. Following the 1977 World Championships in Birmingham, this condition took on almost epidemic proportions with the sudden arrival of the spectacular high-toss service. Thousands of kids up and down the country could be seen at tournaments bravely imitating their Asian idols, throwing the ball up somewhere into the lights, only to make a complete hash of things when it came down.

If only they knew of the hours and hours of practice these Orientals put into perfecting their new technique.... If only the kids could appreciate the years of sweat and dedication they had devoted to acquiring automatic, consistent mastery of the basic strokes before their gurus would let them even *think* about attempting a high-toss service.

The grip

It is impossible to look at stroke play without first giving some thought to the grip.

The grip

The two most popular types of grip in modern table tennis are the western-style 'shakehand grip' and the Asian 'penhold'. The former is simply what its name suggests — shaking hands with the bat handle — with the forefinger controlling the angle of the blade. The penhold grip is quite different, in that only one side of the bat is used to strike the ball. It comes in two variations: the Japanese style, where the thumb and forefinger close around the handle with the remaining three fingers splayed across the back of the blade, and the Chinese style, which is very similar except that the fingers are cupped.

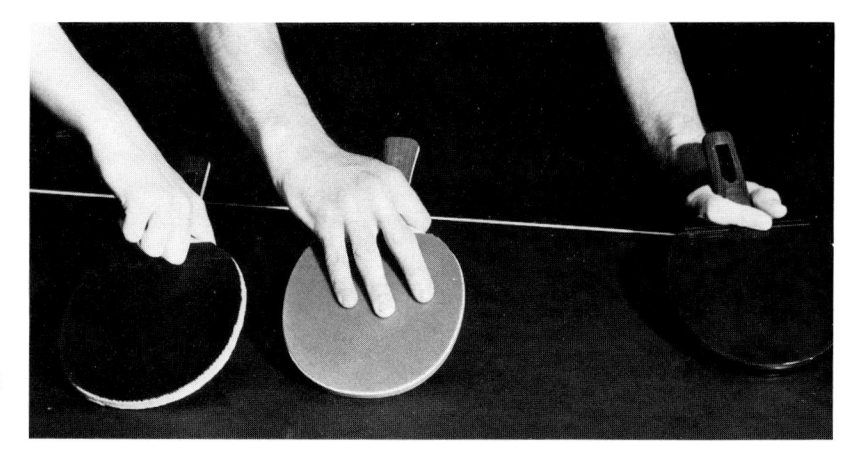

Left to right: Chinese penhold grip with fingers cupped.
Japanese penhold grip with fingers splayed.
Front of bat showing thumb and forefinger common to both grips.

I like to think that there is no one fixed way to hold a table-tennis bat. This is because I have seen so many of today's world-class players holding the bat in their own individual ways. Nobihiko Hasegawa of Japan, World Champion in 1969, held the bat with his forefinger running down the centre of the blade on the backhand side. He was an enormously fit player who based his game around a powerful forehand attack, so it is difficult to assess how much of an advantage this style of grip was to him. One thing is certain, though — that style of grip suited *him*, and he obviously felt it was comfortable.

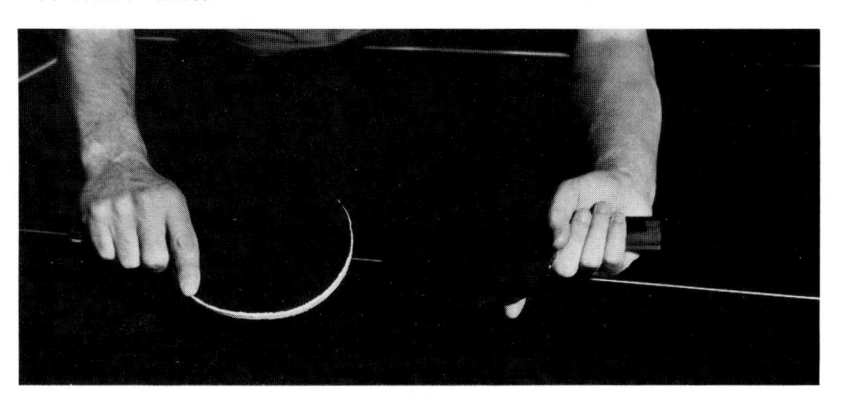

The Western shakehand grip, backhand *(left)* and forehand *(right)*.

3. Getting to grips with the basics

The point I am trying to make here is that we should be open-minded and flexible in our approach to this basic element of the game. What is important is that the grip should be comfortable to the player, and not what the coach *thinks* is comfortable. Naturally, it should not be too tight, as this will later prevent you successfully playing more advanced strokes in which the wrist becomes a vital element. Nor should it be a grip that inhibits or disadvantages you in any way. The only other point I would make is that it should be the *same* grip for both backhand and forehand. Table tennis is a fast game; you need split-second timing, which means that changing your grip mid-point is a very dangerous habit to pick up. However, your grip should be allowed to develop to suit your eventual style of play.

In recent years the Chinese, the world's top table-tennis nation, have significantly moved away from their beloved penhold grip as the only way to hold a table-tennis bat, and their example is being followed by other leading Asian countries. This shift in style could be due to two developments in the 1980s, which made them sit back and think.

Probably the first was the impact of the Hungarians in the 1975 World Championships at Calcutta, when Istvan Jonyer broke the Chinese monopoly by clinching the men's title. With his partner, the flamboyant Gabor Gergely, he also took the doubles; the two were to return to the winner's rostrum in 1979 at P'yongyang, when Jonyer, with Tibor Klampar, enabled Hungary to win the team title. This latter success must have been the hardest medicine of all for the Chinese to swallow. Jonyer plays a powerful attacking game away from the table, and his loose shakehand grip, clutching the bat well down the handle, lends itself perfectly to imparting tremendous spin from both wings. This must undoubtedly have brought home to the Chinese the limitations of their penhold grip.

The other factor must have been the advent of the controversial combination bat, which the Chinese have since used so well. Obviously,

Variations on the shakehand grip, the loose 'Jonyer' style *(left)* and the 'Bengtsson' style *(right)* with the hand at the top of the handle.

The grip

the full potential of this new weapon can only be exploited by using the shakehand grip.

A couple of the leading younger Swedish players have been seen in recent tournaments changing the grip of the bat on their service alone. Doing this enables them to gain maximum relaxation of the wrist and thereby achieve more spin.

Jan Ove Waldner, one of a new breed of Swedish players and runner-up for the 1982 European Men's Singles title at only 16 years old.

The four basic strokes

Almost every other shot in table tennis is based around four strokes: the backhand push; the forehand drive; the backhand drive; and the forehand push. It is a good investment when you are learning the game not to neglect any of these. Concentrate on them all.

If you turn out to be a defensive player, like me, you will still find the ability to hit yourself out of difficult situations invaluable in a match. Likewise, for a strong half-volley player, or 'blocker', it is useful to be able to move away from the table and defend a little if the occasion demands it. I recall seeing Dennis Neale, the former England number one, on many occasions going back and chopping the ball as though he had been doing it for years, particularly when faced with strong topspin opposition.

Timing

There are two schools of thought on the question of timing, which is of key importance in playing the game successfully.

Many coaches and table-tennis luminaries agree with the theory that H. T. Whiting put forward in his book *Acquiring a ball skill*. Mr Whiting maintains that if, when a player starts playing a ball game, he is taught to take the ball early, then that early-timing point will be with him for the rest of his playing days. This may be in spite of the fact that the player has a natural, instinctive tendency to play the ball late; as a defender, I have that tendency myself.

In other words, potential defenders are being conditioned into attacking players because their coaches are encouraging them to take the ball before the peak of its bounce. As a result, they never achieve what they may actually be capable of.

On the other hand, there is a strong body of opinion which maintains that it is the stroke that becomes fixed, and not the timing point. The timing point, it is claimed, will adjust automatically as the young player grows, but the strokes will remain fixed. I do not agree absolutely with either of these theories.

Looking back at when I started playing, I am certain that one of the factors that made me a defensive player was that I simply was not tall enough to take the ball early or at the top of the bounce; hitting the ball late was unavoidable. Even allowing for my own success, I have still to be convinced of the merits of teaching youngsters to play when they can barely see over the table.

This is because I believe that beginners should be able to play the ball at the top of the bounce. Adopting this approach leaves room for players to develop whichever way their natural instincts and personality takes them. If a small child is anxious to play, then try and get hold of a shorter-legged table so that the ball can be played like this. In all of the four basic strokes that we are going to look at now, I have assumed a timing point at the peak of the bounce.

The backhand push

This is probably the easiest stroke to start with, as it allows a beginner to develop that vital asset, ball control.

STANCE: close to the table with your weight slightly forward and on the balls of the feet, which should be about as wide apart as the shoulders. Your shoulders should also face where the ball is to be hit.

BAT ANGLE: slightly open.

THE STROKE: relatively short and played with a pivoting action from the elbow but with little or no wrist movement. The bat moves smoothly downwards, striking the lower part of the ball and literally pushing it over the net. If possible, the point of contact should always be in front of your stomach — so that means moving your feet, rather than stretching your arm.

Study the photographs on pages 24 and 25.

The forehand drive

STANCE: close to the table as in the backhand push, but with the left foot leading the right in a side-to-square fashion. Your left shoulder should be pointing to where the ball is to be hit.

BAT ANGLE: slightly closed.

THE STROKE: played with a pivoting action from the elbow, which is slightly away from the body at an angle of about 120°. Again, there is little or no wrist movement. As the bat moves upward through the ball, the elbow closes to finish at about 90°. The shoulders rotate simultaneously to face square to where the ball is played and the weight is transferred from the right leg to the left.

This stroke is sometimes played with a square stance similar to that described for the backhand push, but it is still important that your shoulders rotate through the shot. Indeed, the Hungarians Jonyer and Klampar play with this very economy of footwork. However, at beginner's level, a side-to-square stance makes the rotation of the shoulders much easier to achieve.

Study the photographs on pages 26 and 27.

The backhand push.   Start.

Contact.

Follow-through and finish.

The shot as seen by the opponent.

The forehand drive.   Start.

Contact.

▲ Follow-through and finish. Note the transfer of weight from the author's right leg to her left.

▼ The shot as seen by the opponent.

Backhand drive and backhand block

STANCE: same as that for the backhand push.

BAT ANGLE: slightly closed.

THE STROKE: pivoting from the elbow, the bat — which starts slightly lower than the elbow — moves upwards through the ball, striking it in front of the stomach. The bat finishes the stroke slightly above the elbow. If you think of the bat and the forearm as the hand of a clock, the movement is from 11.45 to 12 o'clock.

Study the photographs on pages 30 and 31.

It is also appropriate at this point to mention the backhand block, which is very similar to the drive. The only real difference is that the stroke is shorter, with little or no movement, and the ball is taken very early in the bounce. This is a popular and effective defence against heavy topspin and will be looked at later, in more depth, when I come to discuss advanced techniques.

Contact is made early in the bounce.

The forehand push

I have deliberately left this shot until last. Learners have great difficulty in coming to terms with it, so I recommend that perhaps thirty to forty hours' playing time be devoted to the other three first, to acquire the degree of control needed to master the forehand push.

STANCE: same as for the forehand drive.

BAT ANGLE: slightly open.

THE STROKE: like the backhand push, this shot is based almost entirely around a pivoting elbow, with the bat moving slightly downwards through the ball and again, literally pushing it over the net. As in the forehand drive, the shoulders should rotate slightly to finish facing square to where the ball has been hit.

Study the photographs on pages 32 and 33.

Thoughts for the coach

It should usually take about sixty hours on the table for the beginner to become fairly competent at the four basic strokes. It is not crucial that they should be introduced in the order I have set them out.

For example, the Swedish attitude is that attacking shots like the forehand and backhand drive should be the first strokes a new player learns. They claim that at a later stage in the player's life the order of learning will have a strong psychological bearing on their approach to the game. If the push shots are developed first, then these may be the shots the player reverts to if he finds himself under pressure in a big match. However, if the attacking shots are the first strokes to be 'grooved in', then the player will never be afraid of using them and will retain a positive attitude when under pressure.

This is not a theory I entirely support, though I would agree that there is no harm in learning the attacking strokes before the push strokes are developed. But it is important that the beginner is allowed to develop naturally; an inclination to push could mean that there is a promising defender in the making. A game built around defence is now much more of a realistic alternative to attacking than it was about five or six years ago. This is due of course to technological advances in bat rubber, which make it so much easier to contain the fast topspin opponent.

Putting aside the scientific thinking for a moment, it is consistency and ball control that are the beginner's main aims. I have already stressed the need for a solid foundation, and I only wish there was a magic wand I could wave to give this. Life is not that kindly, however, and the only way to success is by good old-fashioned hard graft.

Coaches will probably agree that it is not easy to motivate young players to practise hard at the same strokes for long periods at a time. The Chinese,

Backhand drive and backhand block.

Start.

Contact.

Follow-through and finish.

The shot as seen by the opponent.

The forehand push. Start.

Contact.

Follow-through and finish.

The shot as seen by the opponent.

3. Getting to grips with the basics

though, do not seem to experience much difficulty in applying themselves to the arduous process of 'grooving-in' a shot. Perhaps this has something to do with their vastly different culture. On a number of visits to China, I have always been amazed at their devotion to the game. They will play anywhere, on anything. Both young and old can be seen in the streets playing ping-pong on old sheets of wood propped up at the side of the road with bricks. Young children of eight or nine will shadow play, without a ball, quite contentedly for hours on end.

A youngster well equipped for the game as it was over twenty years ago.

There is no way we could expect our young players to show the same dedication, so remember to make practice as interesting and varied as possible. Young players starting the game can quickly become bored with repeating the same shot over and over. It is always helpful if better players will lend a hand to act as controllers and feed the ball at the same pace to the same area. Keeping the ball going and building up a longer rally boosts enthusiasm.

I would like to finish this chapter by harking back to what I said about copying techniques. Kids have an incredible ability to mimic styles of play, and therefore, if you are a parent who wants to start your youngster playing, remember that the game has changed dramatically in the past twenty years. Gone are the days of Victor Barna, Johnny Leach and even Chester Barnes. It is much faster now, so long follow-throughs with side-on stances are definitely not on.

Quite unwittingly, and without your realising it, your game might look terribly old-fashioned. It is important to see that your protegé is equipped to cope with the way the game is played today.

4 Advanced techniques

Power and spin

When presented with a bag of sweets, a child will almost always pick the ones in the shiny wrappers because they are the ones that are the most attractive and instantly appealing.

Young, developing players, and some who ought to know better for that matter, are very similar. There is little attraction in playing basic strokes such as those we have already looked at; the real thrills lie in the more spectacular and sensational shots. Genuine improvement, though, is very much a gradual process; so, once again, I stress that at least sixty hours table time must be devoted to attaining competence in basic technique before moving on to some of the more advanced strokes we are now about to look at.

It is at this point that we introduce two crucial elements to the top-level game — firstly spin, that devilish ingredient in modern table tennis, and secondly power. Both are closely linked. A whole new host of variations come into play when spin is introduced, and a sound understanding of its effects on the bounce of the ball is enormously important at a higher level. Indeed, I would go so far as to say that a grasp of spin for me has become almost intuitive. Like riding a bike, or driving a car, you know how to handle it without having to think about it consciously.

Power, on the other hand, is a much maligned word, and often wrongly interpreted. In table-tennis terms it means the ability to impart high levels of speed and spin with total control. The key word here is 'control'; for example, to a top player stepping up the pace is similar to a Rolls Royce increasing its speed to 90 mph. Not only does it manage this effortlessly but it can maintain it with ease. A smaller car such as a Mini would not be capable of this and would probably threaten to explode!

Stance — a firm base

Power is generated by transferring body weight through to the shot. Obviously you cannot do this without a firm base from which to operate, so a good stance is vital.

Power and spin

Tibor Klampar of Hungary — a master of the topspin game.

The ready position (frontal).

The ready position (side on).

Stance — a firm base

Unlike other racquet sports, attacking table tennis does not allow players very much time to return to a neutral position between shots, so it is important that the stance adopted allows you to reach any part of the table as efficiently and economically as possible.

The photographs show me in the sort of stance which will help you do this.

As you can see, my feet are about as wide apart as my shoulders with my knees slightly bent. My weight is centred on the balls of my feet, with my heels lightly grazing the floor. My back is arched forward a little so my chin is roughly in line with my knees. From this position it is easy to spring either forwards, backwards or sideways. Also, note the position of my non-playing arm, which is balancing the rest of my body. As we shall see later, the free arm plays a considerable part in helping to rotate the body and transfer weight.

Follow-through — a waste of time?

When the ball is in play it is impossible to readopt every last detail of this stance between shots, so we must look at other areas where we can economise on unnecessary movement.

One such area is the follow-through. Some coaches place desperate importance on a smooth follow-through, which is fine and has my total support. What they often overlook, though, is the length of that follow-through. In percentage terms, the breakdown of a typical forehand drive or, even more significantly, a forehand topspin is invariably as shown in the diagram.

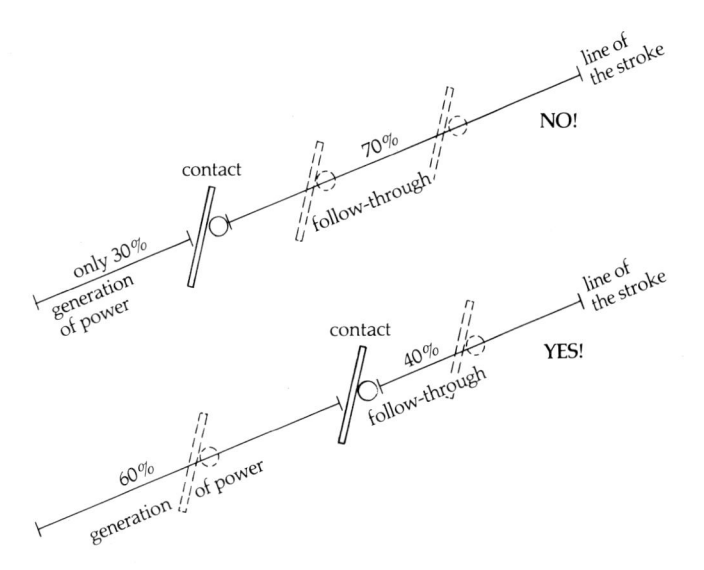

Devote more of the stroke to generating power, and less to a long and wasteful follow-through.

4. Advanced techniques

Some 75 per cent of the shot appears to be a waste of energy, yet the stroke cannot be played with accuracy unless there is some follow-through. To jerk the stroke or try to slow down after contact is both dangerous and difficult. However, I do feel our coaches should be trying to shift the emphasis of stroke production away from the follow-through, and more towards generating the speed of the bat prior to contact.

Slow forehand topspin

STANCE: side-to-square, with the knees bent, as the strength and power of this shot will come from the thighs.

BAT ANGLE: the bat is almost vertical to the table surface.

TIMING: the ball is taken at just above table height, after the peak of the bounce.

THE STROKE: the bat starts from below the knees with the elbow at an angle of about 120°. As the bat moves up to meet the ball, the knees begin to straighten, forcing the body weight upwards from the back foot, which is perpendicular to the line of play. At the same time the elbow starts to close a little immediately before contact with the ball, and the waist and shoulders have rotated to face the line of play. The bat makes contact, swiftly brushing the back of the ball at about 9 o'clock as shown in the diagram.

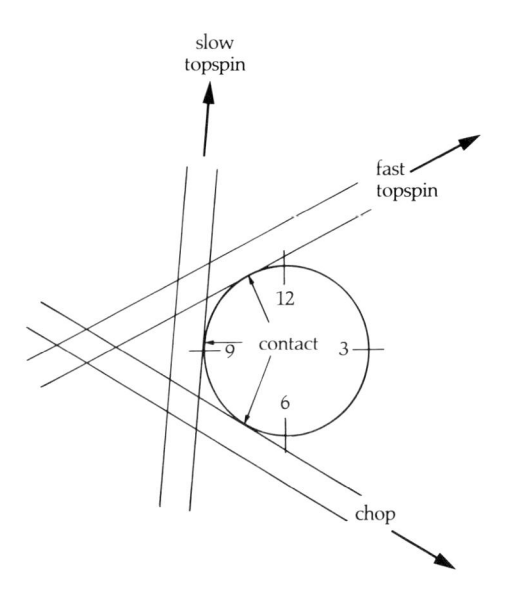

Points of contact. Note that the words 'slow' and 'fast' relate to the speed of the *ball*, not to the spin. The ball spins much faster in the slow topspin, and slower in the fast topspin.

Start, knees bent.

Contact.

Follow-through and finish with the legs straightened.

Start.

Contact. Note the angle of the bat brushing the top of the ball.

Follow-through and finish with the body weight firmly on the left foot.

Fast forehand topspin

STANCE: the same as for the high topspin.
BAT ANGLE: slightly closed.
TIMING: peak of the bounce.
THE STROKE: many features of the slow heavy topspin apply to the fast version. The bat starts just above the knees, which are bent, and further behind the body; however, the rotation of the shoulders and waist is the same. The main difference is that the body weight is forced forward rather than upwards, with the bat travelling in a plane at about 45° to the horizontal. Instead of brushing the back of the ball, the bat makes contact at about 'half past ten'.

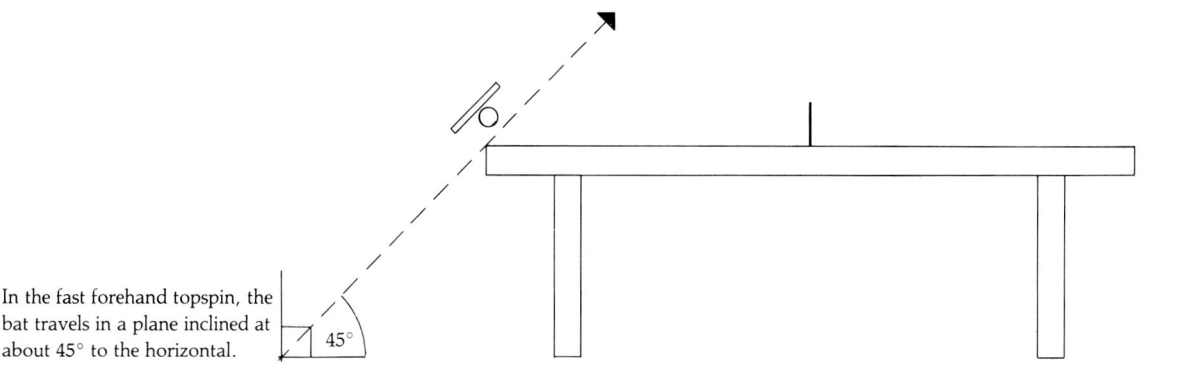

In the fast forehand topspin, the bat travels in a plane inclined at about 45° to the horizontal.

Two integral ingredients in the successful execution of the forehand topspin game remain to be discussed; they are the use of the wrist and the non-playing arm.

It needs to be stressed that maximum spin will only be achieved in the former if the wrist is used on contact with the ball. It is the fastest-moving part of the arm, yet it is the weakest. The action of a good 'looper' is very much like that of a whip. The power is generated in the handle of the whip — the player's legs — and the energy travels along the whip through to the end — along the arm to the bat. Slight movement of a whip handle causes the tip to move at great speed. If the whole arm keeps fluid and the energy generated in the legs travels down the arm and elbow to the wrist, the bat will travel fast enough to impart a high degree of spin. If the wrist remains stiff, however, very little spin will be possible.

The non-playing arm, contrary to first impressions, is a very important factor in the build-up of power. If it is keeping the body in balance, as we have already seen, then it can be used as a major aid to rotation of the waist and shoulders, pulling the weight in the direction required. It is important that the free arm is used to assist the shot and not to hinder it.

4. Advanced techniques

Hungary's flamboyant Gabor Gergely in full flight.

One of the greatest exponents of a powerful forehand topspin that England has seen in recent years is Nicky Jarvis. Nick has now unfortunately retired from competitive table tennis but remains an active force in the game, as non-playing captain of the England Women's Squad.

Variety is the spice of life!

Any player who aspires to play an attacking topspin game must be able to play both the shots I have outlined.

To play a fast loop all the time will only lead to the opponent becoming familiar with the degree of spin on the ball, so the spin must be varied. In considering a subject such as topspin it must be recognised that the bulk of the energy that goes into the stroke is directed to imparting spin, and the remainder into propelling it across the net with a high velocity; the relationship is probably 80 per cent spin to 20 per cent propulsion. With a fast topspin it is much less, probably somewhere in the region of 55 per cent spin and 45 per cent propulsion.

Undoubtedly, the forehand loop is a versatile shot, and I have witnessed further developments of the shot during my career which have made it even more devastating.

Sidespin loop

STANCE: the same as the fast and high topspin.
BAT ANGLE: slightly closed.
TIMING: at or below table height, usually played away from the table.
THE STROKE: the basic principles are the same as for the fast and high
topspin. The real difference lies in the arm action and the position of the wrist, which is dropped so that the bat hangs a little. The bat starts from behind the body and moves in an arc across it, so imparting a side-spinning topspin. *See photograph on page 47.*

Superb artists in this stroke are its inventors, Messrs Jonyer, Gergely and Klampar of Hungary.

There is also the 'off the bounce' topspin, as practised by Tibor Klampar to such great effect. Here the ball is taken straight off the bounce with the bat very much closed over the ball, which is hit at about 12 o'clock. It is a comparatively shorter stroke and is used to counter topspin itself. This is a recent introduction to the European game, and will doubtless work its way into the domestic circuit in the next couple of years — by which time we will be too late again. Shouldn't we be thinking about being the innovators for a change?

It is not only in the area of attack that the loop has been successful. Jacques Secretin has adapted it as a means of defence, lobbing the ball very high with

4. Advanced techniques

plenty of topspin on it, landing it deep in his opponent's half of the table. If the conditions are right, Secretin will fall back from the table and adopt this technique, an aggressive defence, which is not only difficult to kill but can quickly wear down an opponent who may be less than 100 per cent fit.

Jacques Secretin of France, one of the game's most spectacular performers and the authors' favourite player.

Start of sidespin loop.

Backhand topspin

In the early 1970s, the backhand was very much considered as a shot which would contain the game. It was underexploited, and players would always be looking for an opportunity to run round the backhand so as to get in with the more powerful forehand loop.

The Hungarians reconsidered this naïve approach and in the mid-1970s burst onto the scene equally strong on both wings, having developed a backhand loop. It did more than just keep the ball on the table, it forced errors and won points. As a result, the balance was restored and now it is not good enough to be strong on just the forehand; the backhand has to be just as good. Indeed, a few of our top players were caught out by this shift of emphasis. Nicky Jarvis, in particular, found his results deteriorating because his backhand was not strong enough compared with his forehand, and Continental opponents were just the opposite, using a positive backhand loop to deny him the use of his dangerous forehand.

STANCE: square to the line of player, as in the backhand drive but with the knees bent more.

BAT ANGLE: very slightly closed, just off the vertical.

TIMING: after the peak of the bounce, just above table height.

THE STROKE: the bat starts at just below knee height with the wrist lower than the elbow. As the bat moves up to meet the ball, the knees begin to straighten and the angle of the elbow begins to close. The body weight, as in the forehand topspin, is forced upwards. The bat makes contact with the ball, brushing it at about 'half past nine', and the follow-through is smooth but economical.

4. Advanced techniques

Backhand topspin. Start.

Contact.

Variety is the spice of life!

Follow-through and finish.

The start of the backhand loop as seen by the opponent.

4. Advanced techniques

Both Gergely of Hungary and Grubba of Poland play this stroke magnificently; the former adopts a sideways stance so as to rotate the shoulders into the shot as well. This is possible because he is further away from the table and, therefore, has more time. However, it must be stressed that if this technique is used, the player must return to the neutral position so as not to be caught out with the fast ball down the forehand side.

André Grubba of Poland demonstrating his powerful backhand loop.

Backspin — chopping your way to success

Most players these days are 'attackers'. It could even be argued that the English coaching programme is geared toward coaching the 'attacking' game in preference to defence.

Personally, I do not care for the words 'attack' and 'defence' to describe the topspin and chop techniques respectively. Every player should aim to be an attacking player, in attitude at least, irrespective of the technique used. The aim is always to win, so aggression is the key. If you are aggressive and positive about your game, then, in my opinion, you are an attacking player, whether you are looping or chopping.

Twenty-five years ago the balance was quite different. Reverse sponge rubber was still something of a gimmick and its properties had not been fully exploited. Most players played the chopping game and all the greats at the time were choppers — with the odd notable exception, such as Marty Reisman of the USA, who hit fiercely on both wings with the old 'Barna' type bat. When I started playing it was not the fashion of the time that led me to adopt a game based around the chop. It was a style I felt comfortable with, and one which my comparatively short size allowed me to use. Following one's natural inclinations is important, I feel, and our coaches should be wary of producing stereotyped players. It is a point I will return to later.

The author with grim determination, using defence as a means of attack.

4. Advanced techniques

However, the chopping game is still a viable way to get yourself to the top. It has enjoyed a bit of a resurgence since the introduction of the combination bat. Takashima of Japan, Liang Ke Liang of China and his compatriot Tung Ling are all outstanding exponents of chop.

The backhand chop

STANCE: away from the table, depending on the power and length of the opponent's shot. For the right-hander the right foot leads slightly, so the line between the shoulders is the line of play.

BAT ANGLE: slightly open.

TIMING: the ball is taken late, at about table height.

THE STROKE: the bat starts level with the shoulders, with the elbow closed at about 90° or even less. As the bat moves down to meet the ball, the elbow opens and the arm lengthens. The bat brushes down the back of the ball at about 8 o'clock, contact being made outside the body with the shoulders rotating to finish square to the line of play. This is the only backhand shot where I would allow this to happen and it must be remembered that the further away the bat is from the body, the more the control of the shot diminishes.

The forehand chop

STANCE: away from the table, as in the backhand chop, and side to square, as in the forehand drive.

BAT ANGLE: slightly open.

TIMING: same as for the backhand chop.

THE STROKE: the bat starts at about shoulder height with the elbow closed at about 90° or even less. As the bat moves down to meet the ball, the shoulders rotate to transfer the weight from the backfoot and the arm lengthens. The ball is hit at about waist height with the head behind rather than over the point of contact. As with the backhand chop, the ball is brushed at around 8 o'clock. *See photographs on pages 54 and 55.*

I like to remain somewhat openminded on the question of stance for both these strokes. Whilst I play with a side-to-square or even a sideways stance, many of the Oriental choppers play completely square on. This is because they can recover quicker from this position, particularly when the pace is fast and they are closer to the table than they might like to be.

As with the loop, more spin can be generated if the wrist is brought into use, though the general principles of the shot should be mastered first. The wrist gives that added venom which forces errors, and should only snap clean in the split second before the bat makes contact with the ball.

The backhand chop.

Start.

Contact.

Follow-through and finish.

4. Advanced techniques 54

The forehand chop. Start.

Contact.

Backspin — chopping your way to success

Follow-through and finish.

The shot as seen by the opponent.

Christian Martin of France showing good form in this study of the forehand chop.

It is also worth remembering that the degree of backspin will vary according to the bat angle. Maximum chop is achieved when the bat is completely open and the ball is brushed underneath at about 6 o'clock.

To be a master of the chop, though, involves the ability to deceive. In England there are many retrievers, but too few artists. Merely to run around getting the ball back is not good enough. At higher levels, good opposition will quickly become familiar with the degree of backspin on the ball, and you will progress no further. The secret of a good chopper is being able to float. This is being able to simulate a chopping action while at the same time imparting little or no spin. Instead of brushing the ball, the bat moves downwards but hits through the ball making contact at about 9 o'clock. I win many points against loopers in this way, even tempting them with a ball that is a little higher but is floated. As a result they misread the spin, or lack of it, and hit the ball off the end of the table.

Backspin — chopping your way to success

Bat angle for the backhand chop (side on).

Bat angle for the backhand float (side on).

4. Advanced techniques

Contact for the chop as seen by the opponent.

Contact for the float as seen by the opponent.

The forehand kill, the dropshot and the block

Any discussion on advanced technique would be incomplete without mentioning these three remaining shots.

The forehand kill

STANCE: side to square, as in the forehand drive.

BAT ANGLE: closed.

TIMING: peak of the bounce, or wait until the ball drops to such a height that it can be played comfortably.

THE STROKE: the bat must start above the height of the ball and the arm is extended with the elbow at an angle of about 120°. As the bat travels down onto the ball, the weight transfers from the back foot onto the front and the shoulders rotate to face the line of play. There is no spin in this shot and 100 per cent of the energy is transmitted into the ball. Hopefully, the ball will now be dead and will not return. After all, it has been killed as the name of the shot suggests, and this should always be the aim.

Many loopers make a hash of this one simply because they fail to bring the bat to a height above that of the ball before starting the stroke. Consequently, they overhit the end of the table.

The dropshot

This is basically a short push shot, invariably used by attacking players against chop defenders whom they have forced away from the table. It is a touch shot, and requires much judgement and skill if it is to be successful;

Gergely plays a delicate forehand dropshot.

The forehand kill.

Start for the forehand kill: the bat is up in the air and above the ball already.

Contact.

Follow-through and finish.

The forehand kill, the dropshot and the block

Contact for the forehand dropshot. The head is as near to the ball as possible for maximum control.

the danger otherwise is that the ball gets stuck up in the air and is neatly despatched by a swift-footed opponent.

The judgement lies in assessing the degree of backspin on the ball and adjusting the bat angle accordingly. A good dropshot is played from a ball that is chopped short, as it is extremely difficult to play an effective dropshot off a long chopped ball. Ideally, it should bounce at least twice in your opponent's half of the table, so a relaxed grip is essential.

4. Advanced techniques

The block

Some coaches would question the value of the block as a form of advanced technique. They consider it a last-resort shot, a stroke that should only be used to contain the play.

However, I would disagree. One only has to look at the phenomenal success of England's Desmond Douglas to realise that in this game a shot is what you make of it. Allowing for his lightning reflexes and anticipation, he does far more than just get the ball back. On both wings he can force the ball by blocking hard and fast. Yet on other occasions he seems to absorb the pace of the ball by pulling his bat away in the split second of contact. Desmond is a positive attacking player, using what is often considered a defensive stroke.

Contact for the forehand block. The speed and spin of the ball govern the angle of the bat.

1980 European Women's Singles Champion Valentina Popova of Russia — one of the hardest counter hitters in the women's game.

The need to specialise

My international experience has taught me many valuable lessons, but one of the most important is that there is no room at the top for a jack-of-all-trades.

England is extraordinary for turning out young players who can play every shot in the book, and perfectly. The trouble with such all-rounders is that at a higher level their looping is not up to scratch, and their defence will not withstand the pace. It is important, therefore, that natural inclination

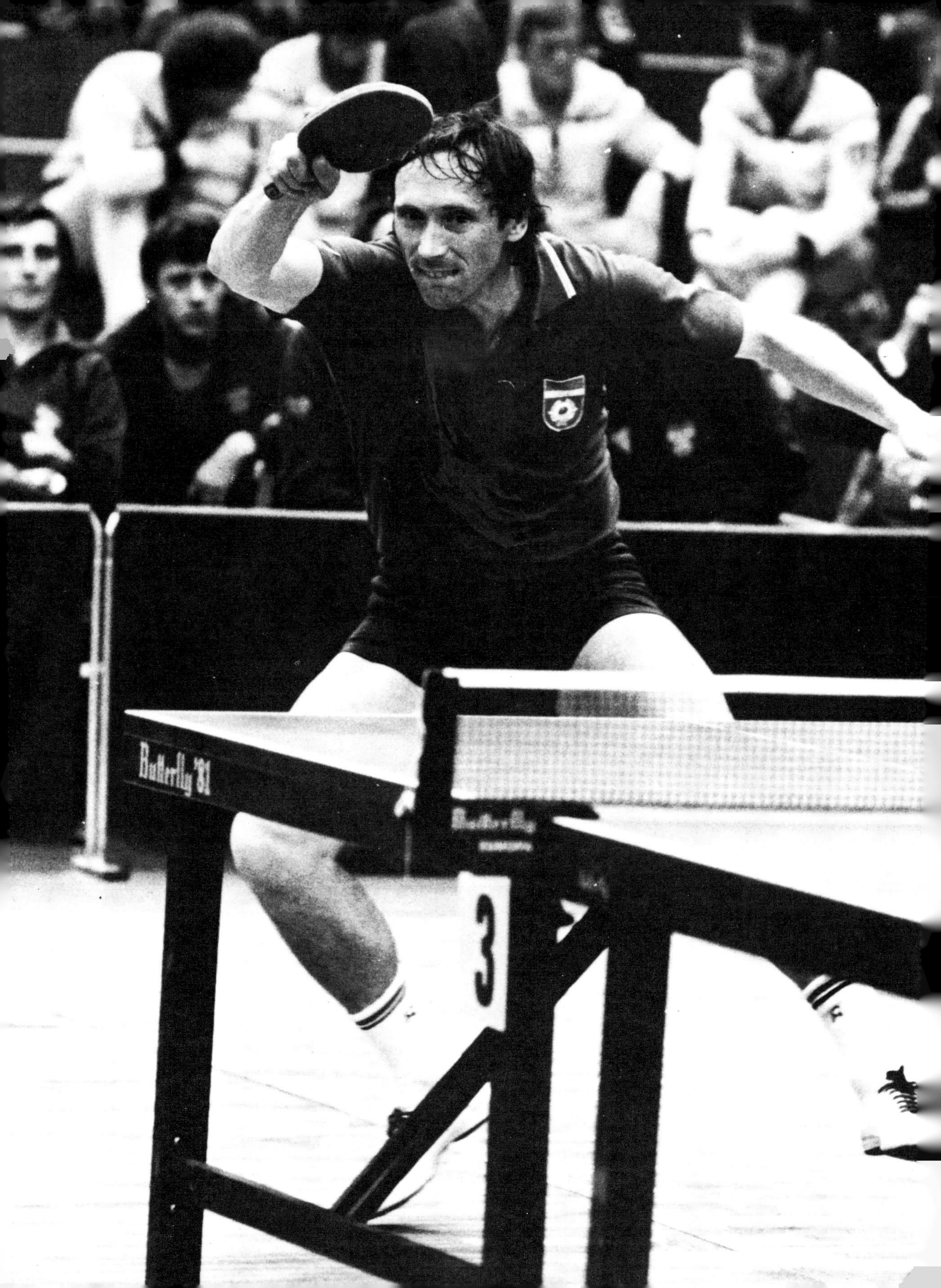
Butterfly '81
3

has its way and — once a general proficiency has been established — a style of play should be adopted. Sooner or later England has got to become the innovator, and not the imitator. All the top international stars are individuals.

Milan Orlowski of Czechoslovakia plays a hard-driving game, picking out the loose ball with ruthless efficiency. Desmond Douglas, as I have just mentioned, is unique in his imaginative use of the block. Dragutin Surbek of Yugoslavia plays a powerful looping game largely based on his forehand from all corners of the table. It is obvious, then, that we ought to allow natural tendencies to develop and that we must not produce stereotyped players.

Dragutin Surbek of Yugoslavia who has been in the vanguard of world table tennis for over twenty years.

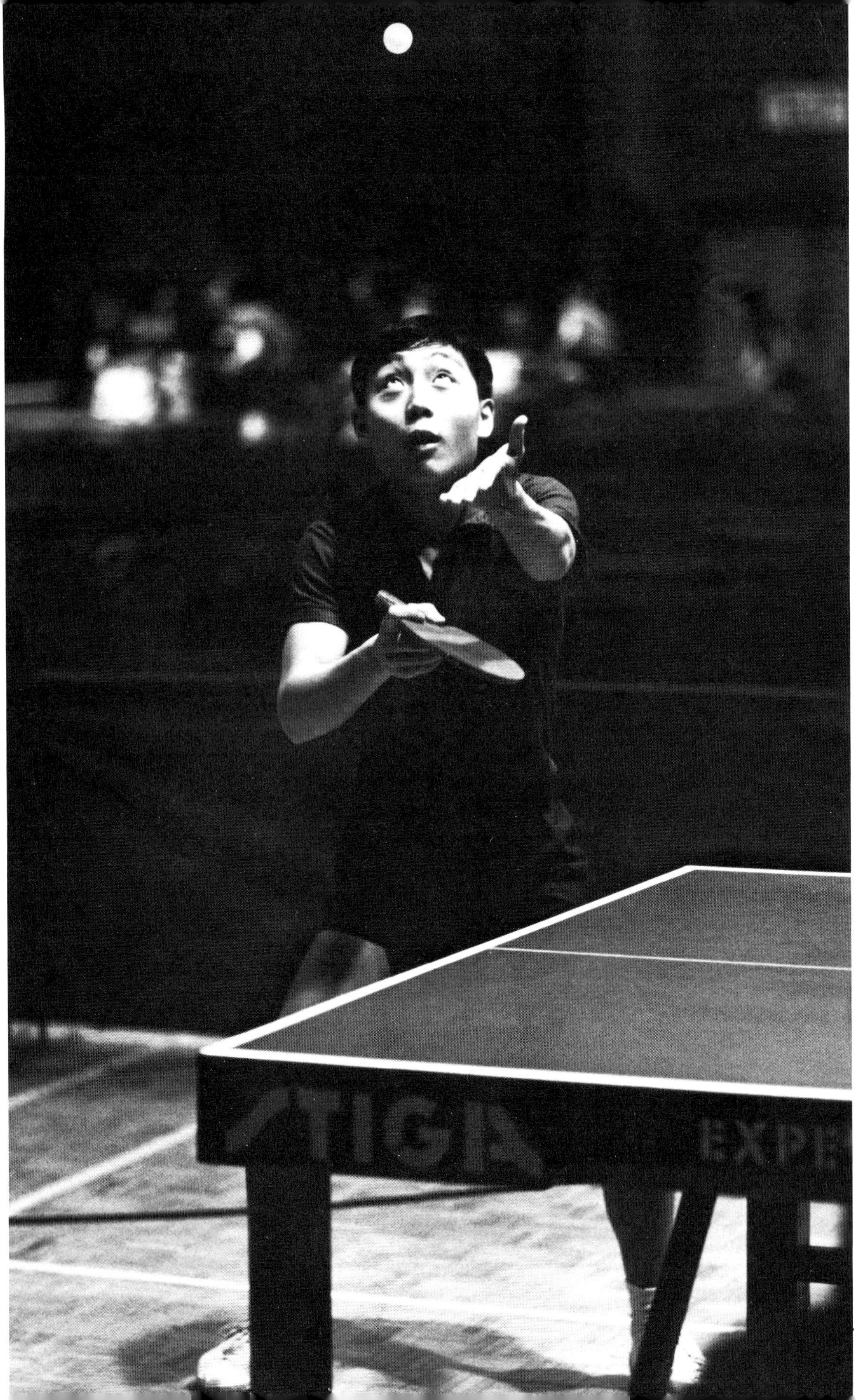
STIGA
EXPE

5 Service and receive

The more I watch — and play against — the Chinese, the more I am conscious how important the service is. At international level now almost 75 per cent of points are over by the fifth ball. We can only conclude from this that the serve is the single most important shot, the receive the second most important, and so on.

The service

Looking at this objectively, the service is the only occasion in the game when you have (or should have!) total control over what you want to do with the ball. This must be an advantage, and we should look upon it in the same terms as the advantage that the server often has in international tennis. Unfortunately, we don't. All too often our younger players see it as nothing more than a means of putting the ball into play. I would estimate that at the point of service a good player has about 70 per cent advantage against the 30 per cent of his opponent. Good serving will put points on to your game.

In the past a number of our more promising players have been awarded sponsorships to enable them to train in Japan for a period of time. Not all of them return as world-beaters, but they invariably come home with a much better service and a more positive receive. You need a lot of application and several hours practice a week to improve your service, and just serving the ball all day can be very boring. The Japanese have overcome this to some degree by inventing a machine (don't they always?) which gathers up the balls served, even those that are caught by the net, and returns them to the player through a series of gulleys and channels.

The short service

Seven or eight years ago, the most popular service in the game was a short service which would bounce three times in the opponent's half of the table. It certainly stopped the receiver getting in with an attacking stroke, but at

Wang of China — one of the most lethal servers in the game.

Takashima, the combination-bat defender from Japan, cunningly conceals his bat prior to serving.

the same time it reduced the server's advantage. The receiver would simply push the ball back, short and very tight, and one was back to square one.

Now the best type of short serve is one which bounces twice on the other side of the table with the second bounce at or about the base line. This retains the advantage and pressurises the receiver. Firstly, it allows more sidespin to be imparted. Secondly, the receiver is unsure whether the ball is coming long and is in two minds about trying to loop it, flick it or attack it in some way. Thirdly, if they decide to push it back they have a far greater distance to play it, which requires great judgement. Instead of the 12 inches or so they would have to cover returning a very short serve, they now have to cope with perhaps three times that distance and still keep the ball short.

Perhaps the best way I can explain how to incorporate these advantages into the short service is to answer some of the typical questions people ask me, when they are trying to improve their service game.

The service

1971 World Champion, Stellan Bengtsson of Sweden. His left foot swings backward at the point of contact to give him good balance for the third ball.

5. Service and receive

Q. How do I get the second bounce near the baseline?

A. You should serve the ball so that it bounces midway on your side of the table. In this way the ball will bounce midway on your opponent's half of the table and the second bounce should then occur near the baseline.

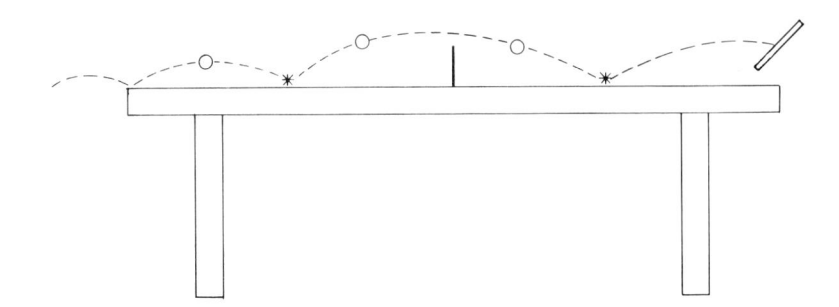

To achieve the 'two-bounce serve', make sure that you strike the ball at the height of the net, and that it bounces midway on your half of the table.

Q. How do I stop my service from bouncing too high?

A. There could be a number of reasons why this is happening. One of the most common faults is for the ball to be hit too high in its descent. Contact should be made at about net height, and this should stop it from bouncing too much. Another reason could be that you are actually hitting the ball into the table and so causing it to bounce up. If this is the case you should check your bat angle, which should be very open, and also the plane along which your bat is travelling. Do not forget you should be brushing underneath and across the ball to generate spin, not pace.

Q. I don't seem to be putting much spin on the ball.

A. This really goes back to my last point. The essence is to convert the speed of the bat into spin. The Chinese are masters at this and their bats travel just as fast when serving short as when serving long. This is because they are brushing the ball, and their bat is accelerating at the point of contact, not decelerating as is often the case with many players.

Q. When I serve short down my opponent's forehand, I often get caught wide down my own forehand side.

A. Firstly, your serve is not as tight as it might be. But the problem could lie in where you are recovering to on the table once you have served. Remember that to serve short down one side opens up an angle for your opponent, as the diagram on page 71 shows.

In this case you should ensure that you move slightly over to your forehand side of table to cover this angle.

The service

To serve short to the opponent's forehand leaves a wide angle to be covered.

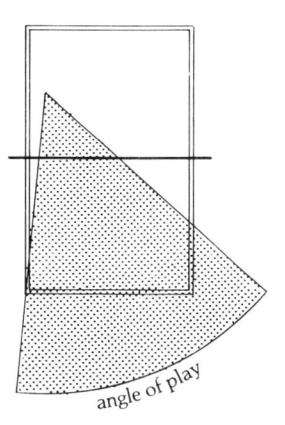

angle of play

Q. Many top players gain great advantage from the high-toss service, but I always seem to make a hash of it!

A. The high-toss service requires great skill and judgement, and to be truly effective it should always be deceptive. As with all services, your opponent should not know where the ball is going until you actually hit it.

England's Paul Day, an accomplished exponent of the high-toss service.

5. Service and receive

To get fine control and more spin, this is one occasion when a change of grip mid-point can be an advantage. Let the handle of the bat drop out from the base of the hand as shown in the picture, so that you are holding the bat loosely between thumb and forefinger with the third finger for balance. Throwing the ball high distracts the opposition because they tend to watch the ball and not your bat. The ball is accelerating on its descent, which should help to put more spin on it. Lastly, brush the ball as close to your body as possible as this will disguise the angle of your bat, making it more difficult for the receiver.

Don Parker gets to grips with this difficult service.

The service

Ulf Carlsson of Sweden showing a good example of a forehand sidespin service. Note the change of grip and how the ball is played from close to his body.

5. Service and receive

The long service

In recent years the long service has become just as popular with some players as its counterpart, the short service. It is only really effective, though, if it fulfils a number of criteria.

Firstly, it must bounce on or about the baseline of the receiver's half of the table. Failure to achieve this will usually mean that the ball is blasted back at you by a very grateful opponent. Secondly, like the high-toss service (which can be short or long, incidentally), you must not telegraph where it is going to go. Your deception should be such that your opponent is left in the dark right up until the point when you actually hit the ball. A good area to place the ball is into the playing shoulder. Finally, if you do opt for a long service it must be fast, or again, the advantage will be lost.

The start of the serve with the ball on the palm of the hand; for the combination-bat player the bat is hidden from the opponent's view.

As seen by the opponent.

Start of the backhand sidespin serve.

Contact.

Follow-through and finish.

5. Service and receive

As a defensive player, I use both long and short services; and using the combination bat I have a lot of variation. I also chop and float the ball on the serve, thinking about the third ball, which is a great opportunity to finish the rally and win the point. Perhaps the best exponent of the third-ball game is Liang Ke Liang of China; his game is largely based around the chop, but nonetheless he will always attack the third ball if the opportunity presents itself.

Contact for the chopped serve (side on).

Contact for the chopped serve as seen by the opponent.

The service

Contact for the floated serve (side on).

Contact for the floated serve as seen by the opponent.

5. Service and receive

Gamesmanship — where do we draw the line?

Gamesmanship plays just as much a part in table tennis as in any other sport. It has its supporters and its detractors. Should we actively encourage it, or should we maintain the typically English attitude of never kicking a man when he's down?

All these points depend very much on exactly where we draw the line between gamesmanship and cheating. Historically, the service has attracted more controversy than any other area of the game. It has forced rule changes; even now the laws of the game relating to service are unclear. In the light of recent developments, perhaps they are in need of further reform. We can only look to and rely on the laws of the game to define what is cheating and what is gamesmanship.

Therefore, it is quite ridiculous when certain foul services are quite rightly ruled against in Britain, but a blind eye is turned to them on the European circuit. My years of experience as a player have taught me to be philosophical about this, but what of our junior representatives? The shortcomings in the attitude of European umpires to the question of foul serving has been brought home to me more acutely since I was appointed as non-playing captain to the English Junior Girls Squad.

England spends a lot of time and money in preparing junior players for foreign championships. Their only competitive experience hitherto will have been on the domestic tournament circuit with English umpires in attendance. Because English umpires are the best in the world, the player knows exactly what is permissible in the service. It seems terribly wrong, then, that when they arrive on the European continent they can be put out of the event by a foul serve, never having been given the chance to compete properly. Regretfully, our attitude now is to teach our players that in Europe anything goes unless the umpire says otherwise.

On the other hand, there have been instances when I could only admire the way foreign opponents have exploited the laws, but in the spirit of the game. One occasion that springs to mind was at the 1982 European Youth Championships at Hollabrun, in Austria. The game in question was between Nicky Mason of England and Johnny Akesson of Sweden, in the semi-final of the Boys Team Event. Mason was leading 19—16 in the first game and Akesson was about to serve.

In a brilliant fit of imagination, young Akesson served each of the five services from under his right leg! Everything conformed to the laws of the game, and the ball was visible all the time. Amazed, Nicky proceeded to lose the next five points and the game because he was too busy watching the player and not the ball and bat.

Receive of service

In theory, at least, we have already seen that the server should have the advantage, and at higher levels of competition this invariably is the case. But what of the receiver? It is equally important to be able to receive service in such a way that you don't add to the server's initial advantage.

We must return, therefore, to one of the fundamentals of good table tennis: the stance, which we looked at in chapter 4. In between every point, when receiving service, it is essential that the basic stance is adopted if you are to have any chance of receiving the ball well. As we have already seen, this stance should enable you to reach any part of the table quickly. I am often asked exactly where on the table the receiver should be positioned; the only answer I can give is that the receive position should be facing the opponent, with the bat pointing to the ball, and standing in a position that suits your style. The diagram explains this.

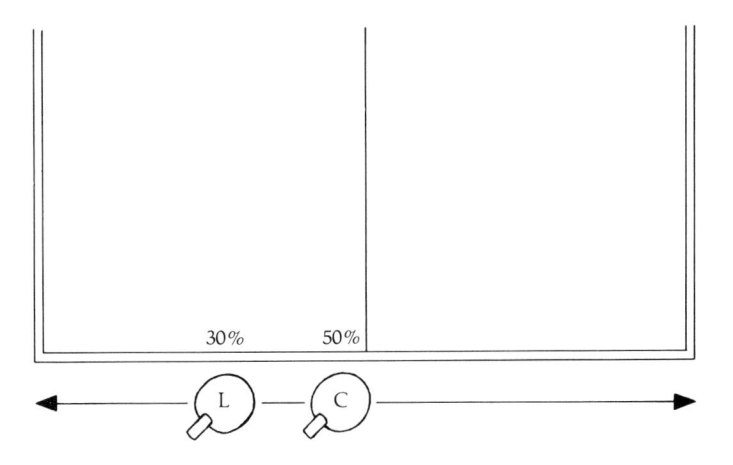

As a rule, the looper (L) tries to cover some 70% of the table with his forehand, whereas the chopper covers 50%. But remember, when receiving service the bat is held over the right leg, so the body will be to the left of the bat positions shown here.

Of course, this will vary depending on where the server stands. If you are a forehand-oriented player you should stand to the left of centre of the angle of play; this will shift according to where the server is positioned, which means that you must reposition yourself accordingly.

5. Service and receive

The receiver must position himself just to the left of the angle of play. This will vary somewhat, according to where the serve comes from.

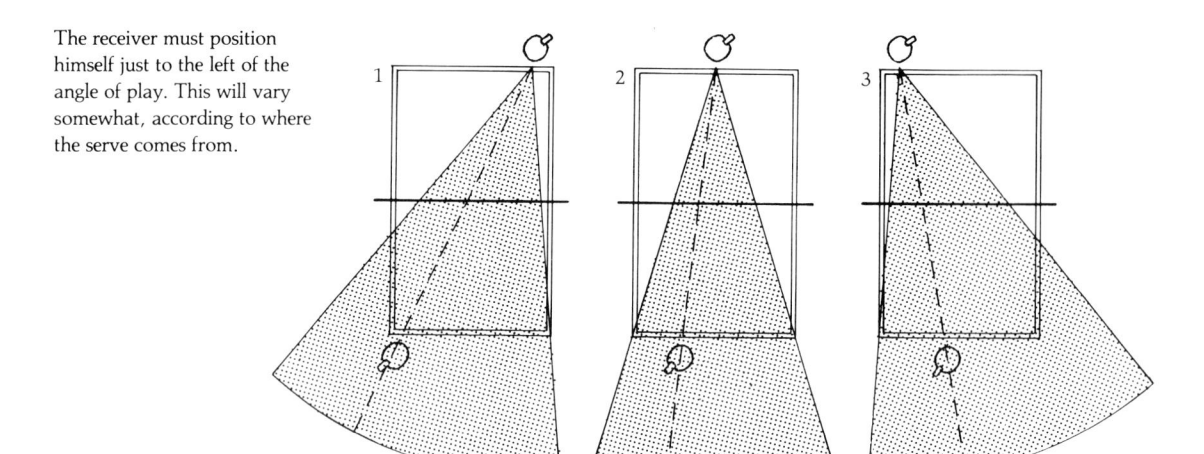

As a predominantly defensive player, I favour a fifty-fifty position between backhand and forehand, but again this will depend on the server's possible angle of play. In addition, I like to be able to touch the end of my bat on the table with my elbow at an angle of about 90°.

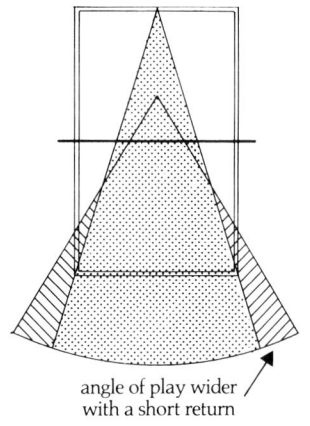

Remember: the deeper you can return the ball, the narrower will be your opponent's angle of play.

angle of play wider with a short return

I have already mentioned the dangers of only watching the ball (see pages 72 and 78). If you are to gain some idea of the direction, length and type of spin on the ball it is important that you should watch your opponent's bat and not be distracted by anything else.

At the turn of the 1970s, the Japanese seemed to be masters of nimble, efficient footwork, particularly so on the receive of service. Playing, as so many of them do, with the limited penhold grip, they would deliberately position themselves well over to the left of the table so as to maximise the use of their powerful forehand attack. Incredibly, though, they never seemed to get caught out wide down the forehand.

Developments in the game seem to have overtaken them a little, and it is now very difficult to succeed unless the backhand is very strong as well. Having trained in Japan and closely watched this technique on receiving service, I still feel that it is very limiting. There is no need for a player with the Western style of grip to adopt a position of receive so far over to the left of the angle of play.

However, the Japanese do seem to have left us with some valuable guidance on how to economise on footwork in this crucial area of the rally.

Receive of service

Milan Orlowski of Czechoslovakia well poised to receive service.

Watching their technique and that of other leading players, my advice is as follows:

- If the serve is long to the forehand, then with simple, stepping footwork an attacking player should try to topspin the ball back.

- If the serve is long to the backhand, then again a backhand topspin should be played, with feet square to the line of play. (On both wings, as a defender, I might possibly seek to chop or float the ball deep, perhaps into my opponent's playing shoulder.)

- If the ball is short to the backhand then it can be flicked or pushed back short. If you decide to flick it (on either forehand or backhand) it will not be sufficient to just get under the ball and roll it over. The bat must make contact at the back of the ball and flick it hard.

Two methods for receiving a short serve to the forehand — the Japanese *(left)* and the Western *(right)*. Choose the one that suits you best and with which you feel most comfortable.

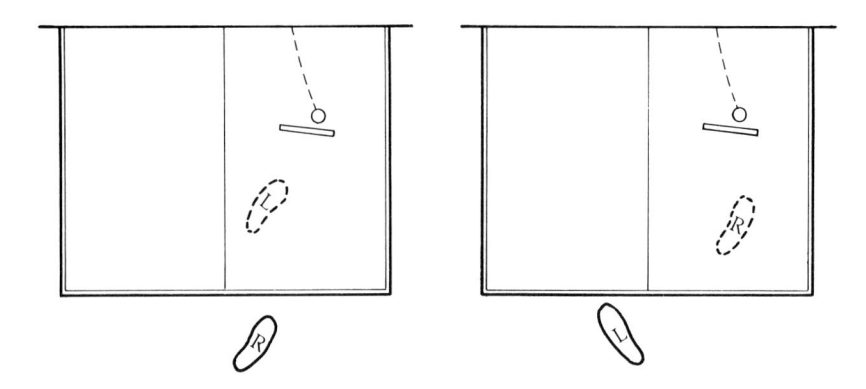

- There only remains the short ball to the forehand. In my opinion, there are two ways of playing this. Both have their advantages and disadvantages, and players must choose the technique that suits them the best.
  1. The Japanese will invariably step across with the left foot, which goes under the table. From here either a push or flick is played. However, from this position it is easy to step back if you have misjudged the ball and it happens to be long. But it is also very difficult to recover if the serve is switched at the last second to the backhand.
  2. The second approach is to play with the right foot under the table. This is a good position from which to recover to the backhand and it also brings your head nearer to the ball, which will help in controlling it. However, it is not easy from this position to retreat if at the last minute the serve is played long and fast down the forehand.

Receive of service

Danny Seemiller of the USA receiving serve with a delicate forehand push; by keeping his head near to the ball he can maintain good control.

The one factor characterising all these answers to the various serves is that each of them involves a positive shot. A pushed ball is positive if it is close to the net and short, as it is taking some of the advantage away from the server. Topspinning is positive, as is a well-placed chop; but above all do *something* with the ball! To just roll it or half hit it will only ensure that you are under pressure for the remainder of the point.

My final comments on receiving service concern what area of the bat you use; this is certainly worth giving some consideration to. The centre of the bat offers the most control, and this is the best part to use when controlling a short fast-spinning ball. Equally important to a 'looper' is that the outer part of the bat is the fastest moving part. When dealing with (loose) long serves, the topspinner should be trying to use this part of the bat for that extra bit of spin.

6 Footwork

Good footwork is as important to a table-tennis player as it is to a boxer, except that in table tennis you will not get punched in the nose if you fail to move fast enough. You just seem to lose more games. It is fleetness of foot that has helped make Muhammad Ali a legend in our lifetime, and an unscarred one at that. Would-be table-tennis players should take a leaf out of his book. Many technical problems are wrongly diagnosed, when in fact the root of the problem is footwork.

Basically, footwork is used as a means of enabling a player to repeat exactly his established dominant stroke from any position on the table — in other words, to get to the ball to play the shot. Now, I readily concede that this is no earth-shattering deduction, but it is amazingly hard to overcome the temptation to stretch to the ball rather than move there first. This is a natural tendency, so attaining this fundamental principle of good footwork involves hard work. Remember, if you are in the right position, it is very much easier to transfer power and direction into the shot and so play the ball correctly.

Four factors are essential pre-requisites to efficient footwork: footwork patterns, fitness, anticipation and recovery positions. Fitness is dealt with in more detail in chapter 8; suffice it to say here that it is an essential ingredient: you have to be moving as nimbly and swiftly in the fifth game as you were in the first. I have already touched upon the question of recovery positions in chapter 5, but I propose to amplify it a little later on.

Types of footwork

Taking footwork patterns first, these are the established movements a player will make to get to a ball. I use the word 'established' deliberately because that is just what they are — patterns of foot movement which are automatic responses to a given situation. You should not have consciously to think how you are to get to the ball; you should be able to do it without thinking. It is obviously important, then, that these patterns are 'grooved' into the aspiring player as soon as he or she has grasped the basic shots. The

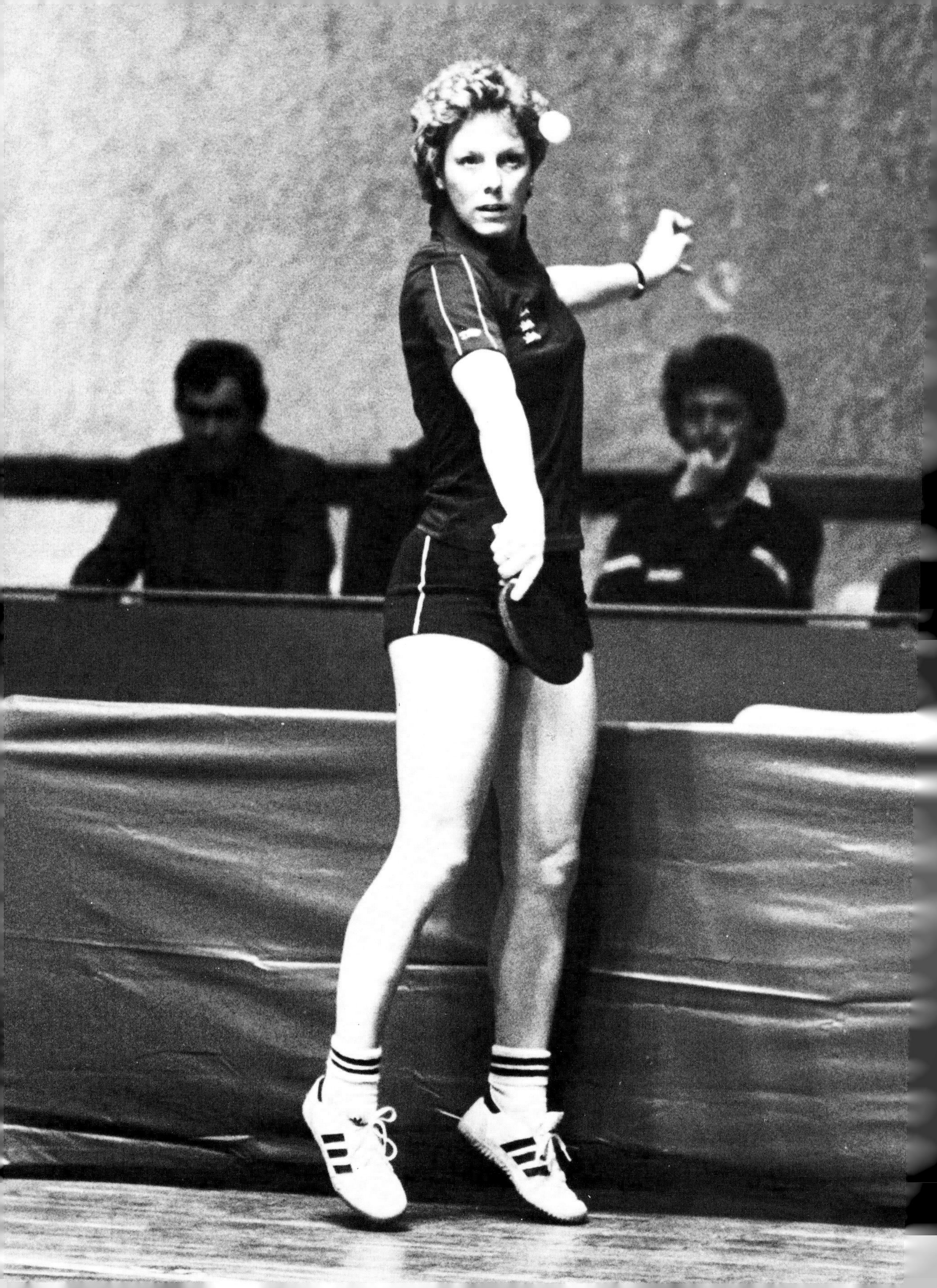

Types of footwork 87

◀ The author with her back to the ropes.

▲
Stellan Bengtsson of Sweden. A superb example of a player who makes it look easy through nimble footwork.

6. Footwork

Gergely of Hungary has unorthodox but nevertheless effective footwork.

best way to do this is by using what the coaches call 'regular footwork exercises'.

In simple terms, these are exercises in which the player knows where the ball is going. A typical example would consist of three balls down the backhand and then the fourth down the forehand; this cycle is repeated over and over. I am a great believer in the inherent natural ability of the individual, so I would stress that there is no fixed way to move across to, say, the forehand from the backhand wing. As long as the player moves quickly and comfortably with no obvious inhibitions to where the ball is and then plays the stroke in the correct fashion, then this is fine. However, the coach should always be on the lookout for the most economical way of achieving this — for example, where two steps will do and yet five steps are being taken.

Close to the table, the best type of footwork is stepping or skipping sideways. It is important, though, that the feet do not cross one another. This will only lead to losing that firm base that we looked at in chapter 4. Also, if the right foot has crossed the left in moving over to the backhand side of the table, it will be very difficult to recover to the forehand side with the body committed in this fashion.

Away from the table, however, it is very difficult to move swiftly without crossing the feet, so a form of running footwork is obviously the best solution. However, I would stress that in moving over to the forehand side the feet should finish in the correct manner, with the left leading the right (in the case of a righthander). The same principle applies on the other wing, where the feet should be square; or when chopping the ball, with the right foot leading slightly. In both these footwork patterns, it will help a great deal if the weight remains on the insides or the balls of the feet, making it easier to spring away. Also, the head and feet should move before the playing arm, and it is better if the eye level is the same throughout.

The next stage is to check that these regular footwork patterns are automatic, whether close to or away from the table. As I have already said, this state of automation is essential to successful matchplay. The best way to do this is through the use of 'irregular' footwork exercises, in which the ball's direction is switched but the player does not know when. Some typical examples are shown in the diagrams.

Irregular footwork exercises.
1. Backhand drive to forehand block, with the switch (S) at random across to the forehand.
2. Backhand drive to backhand block, with the switch again at random to the forehand.
3. Forehand topspin to forehand chop, with the switch at random down the backhand or the dropshot (SD) just over the net.

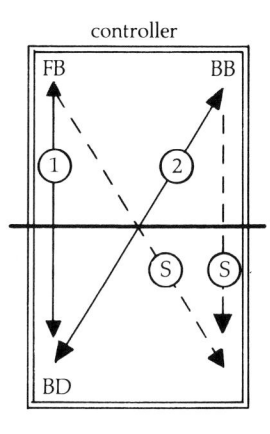

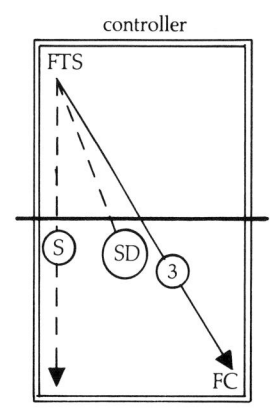

Anticipation and recovery

It is impossible to talk about good footwork and how to go about improving it without mentioning anticipation. As far as the table-tennis player is concerned it is undoubtedly a magic ingredient. It can mean the difference between being unfit but fast and supremely fit but slow. Unfortunately, it is not something I can give you through these pages. Some people anticipate well and have good, almost reflex, reactions and others are less well blessed.

I will give you an example which illustrates this. A few years ago at an England training camp we were training under the direction of Wilf Paish, who is a renowned and respected British Amateur Athletics Association Coach. His speciality in the throwing events has been quite instrumental in the career of shotputter Geoff Capes. Nevertheless, he is an accomplished all-round physiologist.

He was quick to recognise that dynamic strength in the legs — the ability to move quickly over a short distance — is of great use to the table-tennis player. To test our bounding ability, which is a measure of dynamic strength in the legs, and to see how much training we needed in this area he used a standing broad jump. Basically, this is standing and throwing the body forward in one jump. Wilf had gone so far as to develop a scale of measurement out of a hundred based on his testing of international athletes. He used this with us, even though we were only table-tennis players.

My jump was marginally less than average on his scale but would have been quite respectable compared with jumps by a cross-section of most types of sportsmen and women. Then Desmond Douglas jumped and got about mid-way on the scale — quite good. Then Nigel Eckesley went, and his jump went right off the end of the scale! Amazed, Wilf Paish made him repeat it to check that his calculations were right. Again, Nigel leapt off the end of the scale and recorded a standing jump that compared with a similar standing jump by Lynn Davies, the British gold-medal long jumper in the 1964 Tokyo Olympics.

Nigel is enormously strong, very fit and trains exceptionally hard. Not that Desmond is any less dedicated, as he is no mean sprinter himself, but he is not the athlete that Nigel is. However, on the table Desmond Douglas has the fastest reflexes in the world and seems to know where the ball is going even before the opponent hits it. Nigel, on the other hand, is nowhere near as fast in his reactions. He is not blessed with the same gift of anticipation that Desmond has.

It *is* possible to improve your anticipation a little, even though I cannot tell you how to get the lightning reactions of Desmond Douglas. Firstly, try not to watch the ball exclusively. Many coaches I come across are always

Sweden's leading lady of the
1970s, Anne Christine
Hellmann.

shouting at their players to keep their eye on the ball. Well, obviously this is important, but doing it at the expense of all else means that you can only start moving *after* the ball has been hit. Equally important is to develop the ability to watch your opponent and his bat, so you can start moving as the ball is hit or just before. Being a ball-watcher is like giving someone a two-second start in a 100-metre sprint.

The other way to improve movement is to understand angles of play and adopt good recovery positions. We have looked at this in relation to the service and receive, where it is particularly crucial, but the principles apply throughout the remainder of the point. Where to recover on the table is entirely dictated by where you hit the ball, which in turn gives your opponent an angle of play. The precise position for recovering also depends very much on your style of play, but it is almost always slightly to the left of your opponent's angle of play.

The most extreme position I would advocate would be about 70 per cent covering the forehand and 30 per cent covering the backhand. Then again, there are players of the calibre of Grubba of Poland who is exceptionally strong on the backhand. He covers perhaps 50 per cent of the table, if not more, with this side. The main problem with using the backhand excessively, though, is that it is much harder to reach the ball on this side — the arm can always stretch further on the forehand side.

Finally, the bat should always travel through the neutral position, as shown in my discussion of stance in chapter 4. Doing this leaves all your options open to move at speed to any area of the table. After all, this is one of the basic reasons why good footwork is essential — being in the right place to play the right shot.

7 Successful doubles play

With singles often being the most prestigious table-tennis event to take part in and hopefully win, doubles usually gets pushed into the background. As a result, our attitude and our chances of success are poor when it comes to team matches.

In European League matches, doubles sets account for three of the seven games played. In the Corbillion Cup, which is the women's team event of the World Championships, the doubles set is crucially important; with two in a team where everyone plays each other the doubles can often become the deciding set. I have no doubt that this is the case in many local league matches as well. With a little bit of thought and planning I am sure we could all be a lot more successful in doubles.

Stippancic *(left)* and Surbek *(right)* of Yugoslavia, former World Doubles Champions.

Jill Hammersley and Desmond Douglas, USA Open Mixed Doubles Champions in 1976.

Picking your partner

Some players are very choosy about the style of player they are prepared to partner. There are certain styles which do not blend together well, but then again, World and European champion pairs in this event have included every possible permutation at one time or another.

Naturally two attackers make a good pair, as do two defenders or two blockers. But a defender and a blocker can sometimes be a more useful combination. One of my best doubles partners has been Linda Jarvis, who recently retired from the game. She blocks the ball very well and, like me, she is an absorber of spin and pace. Our combination worked so well that we were European Doubles Champions in 1976. When she played with Desmond Douglas in mixed events she was just as effective for the same reasons.

Jill Hammersley and Linda Jarvis en route to the 1976 European Women's Doubles title.

The combination of blocker and attacker, however, is not always successful, purely because the attacker is not as good at absorbing pace and spin as the blocker. This occurs when the blocker half-volleys the ball back to a topspinner in the opponent's team, who returns it to the attacker heavily looped. For the same reasons the combination of attacker and defender is a difficult one to play in.

Gergely and Jonyer of Hungary — one of the game's most powerful loop drive combinations.

There is also the question of whether your partner should be a righthander or lefthander. For two forehand-oriented players, a right/left pairing is a good one for the simple reason that it allows them to cover most of the table easily with their forehand, as the diagram shows.

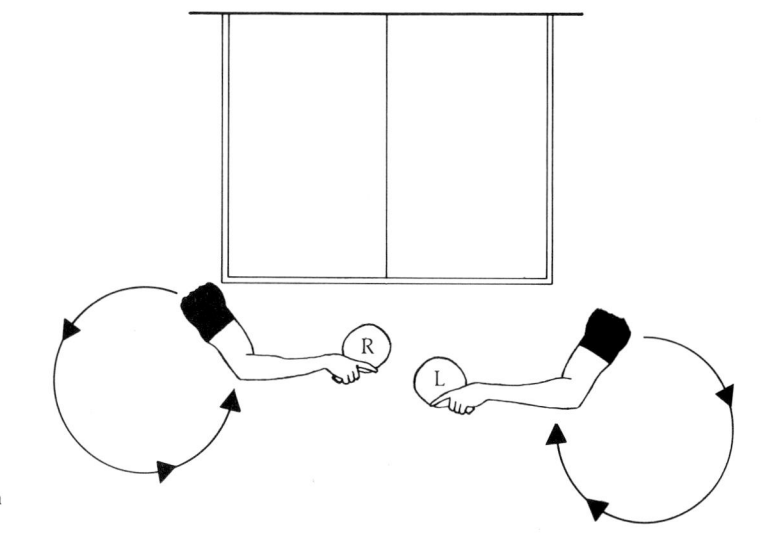

Lefthander and righthander. Both players serve with their forehands. The righthander moves out to the left after playing a shot; the lefthander moves out to the right. In this fashion both players are covering most of the play with their forehands.

7. Successful doubles play

Graham Sandley *(left)* and Douggie Johnson *(right)* of England. An unusual partnership of combination-bat defender and fast attacker.

The righthander takes up a position to the left hand side of the table and the lefthander to the right. It is easy for both players to keep out of one another's way as this position allows such an economy of movement.

A pairing of two lefthanders is also a useful one. The diagram shows the basic tactics to be adopted here. Again, it is relatively easy for both players to keep out of one another's way.

Two lefthanders.
Both players serve with their forehand, and move out backwards to the left once they have played their shot. This system again allows both players maximum use of their forehands.

Picking your partner

It is not as easy for a combination of two righthanders to enjoy such a free use of the table with their forehands. Because the laws of the game say you have to serve from the right (and this particularly suits the previous two combinations), the server in this combination must, having once served, move out to the right before circling around the back of the table so as to come in with his forehand. To move to the left across the table is very risky as it may temporarily block his partner's view of the direction of receipt of service. The diagram below explains how the two right-handed players, from serving or receiving, can recover to a circling technique which will allow them maximum use of their forehands.

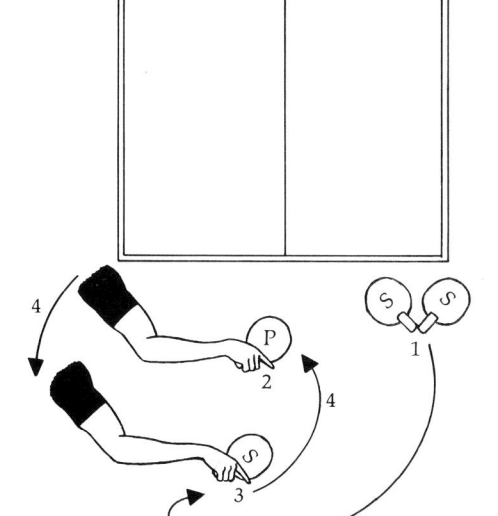

Two righthanders.
1. The server (S) serves either forehand or backhand, and moves out backwards, circling around to the left-hand side of the table.
2. The partner (P) plays the third ball and moves out to the left.
3. The server comes in to take the fifth ball and then moves out to the left.
4. The pair continues in this circular fashion which lets them cover most of the play with their forehands.

Finally, one or two tips about doubles tactics. Make sure your partner knows the sort of serve you are going to play. So you do not have to whisper and possibly tip off your opponents, devise a system of signalling from under the table. Your partner will then know roughly what sort of return to expect.

While on the question of serving, it is not always wise to serve long. This is because of the fact that you must serve from the right into your opponent's right half of the table. Your chances of surprising the receiver with a long serve are reduced because of this reduced target area.

Remember that the order of receiving serve alters when the score reaches 10 in the third game. Your partner may be looping the ball well against a defender, but when you are both forced to change it will be you receiving from that player. Be sure to take account quickly of any change in pace and spin.

The author and Linda Jarvis in action for England.

By taking up a position to the left of the table, Linda is ready to come in with her forehand.

Successful doubles partnerships do not happen overnight. Get to know your partner and play together regularly, developing a rapport between you. Know one another's strengths and weaknesses, and how to avoid exposing one another to difficult returns.

Lastly, do not get upset with your partner even though he or she might be making the more mistakes. You are a team, and anything that undermines your partner's confidence will do your chances no good at all. Words of encouragement are always better.

Secretin and Birocheau of France — European Champions 1980.

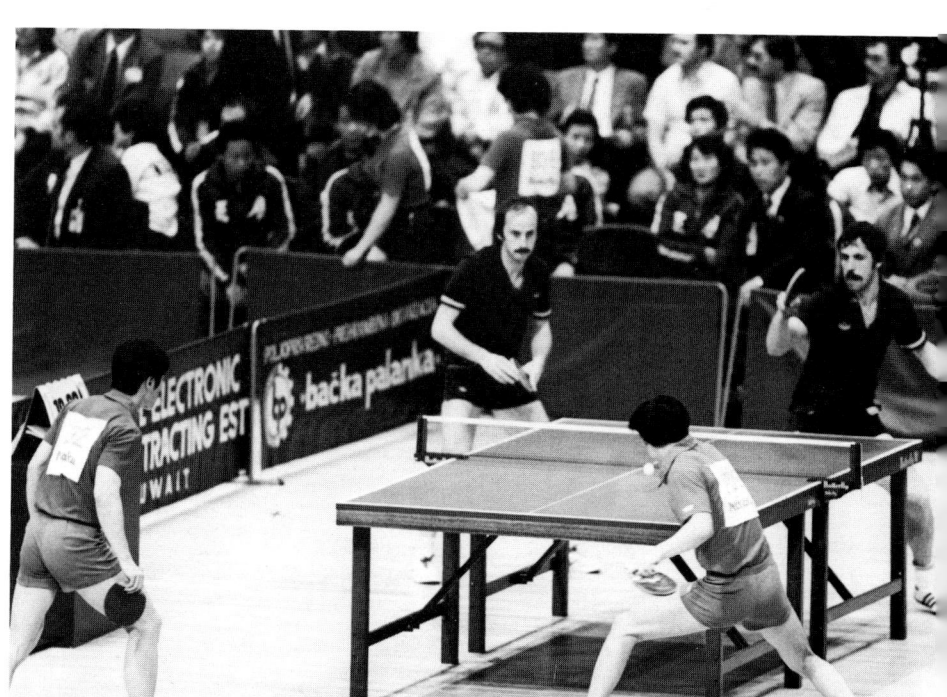

Secretin (left) and Birocheau (right), in action against an Asian penhold combination.

Milan Orlowski of Czechoslovakia — one of the fittest competitors on the world circuit today.

8 Healthy body, healthy game

Table tennis is often considered to be the sort of game for which you do not necessarily need to be physically fit. Of course, this is usually the view of someone who has dabbled in 'ping pong' at the local youth club, and I would agree: there is no need to be fit to play 'ping pong'.

However, it is a different story at the other end of the scale. At international level, you cannot get by without being exceptionally fit. While skill is undoubtedly the most important factor, fitness can sometimes be the decisive factor in a game. Generally speaking, the higher your standard of play, the greater is your need to be fit.

As a defender, it is vital for me to be able to sustain the effort of moving in and out of the table continually throughout a match. In a tournament, I can be involved in several matches in a day. In an event such as the European Championships, days can run into a week or more and at this level, in the individual events, the sets are the best of five games.

Training for table tennis

Like any other sport, fitness training is specific. In other words, we isolate the physical attributes needed by the table-tennis player and build them up. Our training would not, for example, be the same as that for the track athlete, or even the tennis player.

My training programme and that of a lot of my colleagues is generally broken down into four areas: cardiovascular endurance, such as long-distance running; muscular endurance, which is usually a circuit of exercises such as press-ups, sit-ups, squat thrusts etc; flexibility, through the use of stretching exercises; and, finally, exercises to improve dynamic strength, such as bounding and sprinting.

If we look at the physical requirements of table tennis it will become apparent why these types of training are the most suitable.

- The majority of points last around 3—4 seconds, so each one is generally a very short explosion of activity — hence the need for

8. Healthy body, healthy game

dynamic strength in the legs to propel the body quickly about the table and playing area.

- A single game lasts around 5–10 minutes and a best of three anything between 10 and 25 minutes. To maintain this dynamic strength, therefore, we need an element of muscle endurance which helps the body to sustain the effort.

- A match or tournament day can run from about 5 to 15 hours. You will have to be going strong at the end, particularly if you reach the final. Hence the call for muscular and cardiovascular endurance, and the need for flexibility to prevent stiffening up between encounters.

Stamina

Stamina is also referred to as cardiovascular endurance, which means, basically, getting the heart and lungs to work more efficiently. I find the best way to do this is to go running for about 15 to 20 minutes. England senior male squad members are expected to achieve a 2-mile run in 12 minutes. At county level or even town team level, players should be able to cover 1.75 miles in the same time. Stamina is important and it is worth remembering that when your heartbeat exceeds 120 beats per minute, your skill level declines. If the stamina level is high, then the heartbeat will recover more quickly from periods of exertion and the risk of error should diminish.

Muscular endurance

Here I am with some other international players demonstrating the exercises that comprise a typical circuit on one of our training camps.

You can assess your own endurance by choosing five or six exercises, along the lines of those shown. See how many of each you can do in a minute. The circuit will be half the number of repetitions — 'reps' — of each exercise that you achieved in the minute, three times round. You should then time yourself and monitor your progress with a view to reviewing your 'minute' tests and so increasing the reps of each exercise on your circuit. You could even increase the number of exercises.

Some people prefer to use weights to improve their strength in this department. Weight training is undoubtedly an excellent aid but it does need strict and expert supervision. On one training camp a number of the players sustained badly pulled and strained muscles because the coach did not fully appreciate the correct technique of weight training. I would certainly not advocate its use by junior players, as their bodies are still developing and their skeletal structures are not yet fully formed.

▲ *Left to right:* press-ups, squat thrusts, sit-ups, star jumps.

▼ *Left to right:* back arches, side stepping between two points, burpees, heel raises.

8. Healthy body, healthy game

Flexibility

It is always better if the body is supple and flexible. Then the muscles can do their job properly.

An important point for you to remember is to stretch slowly and not to jerk — otherwise you will pull a muscle and that will keep you out of the game completely. The best way is to stretch slowly as far as possible and hold the position for a second or two, then try to stretch further. Usually, if 'warned' in this fashion, the body will respond and allow further movement. Hold this for a further five seconds and then relax. The photograph shows some useful stretching exercises particularly suited to the needs of the table-tennis player.

Dynamic strength

Bounding exercises, such as the one pictured here, will help provide dynamic strength in the legs. This can be measured simply enough, by monitoring the length of one single jump from a stationary position over a given number of weeks.

Shuttle running or sprinting is another method. Sprinting a short distance — say 20 metres, with a 20 second rest in between each sprint — 20 times will improve the dynamic strength in the legs.

One of the fastest sprinters we ever had in the England team was Denis Neale, who represented his country for nearly fifteen years. I remember on one occasion we were flying abroad and we happened to be sharing the same plane as some members of the England Athletics Team. One of their women sprinters passed a disparaging remark about the physical standards needed for table tennis, to the effect that Denis could not possibly be considered an athlete in terms of fitness. Denis proceeded to challenge her to a 100-metre sprint across the tarmac, giving her a 10-metre start. She accepted — and was soundly beaten, much to the other athletes' amazement.

The warm-up

How many times have we heard the desperate cry of 'I was 10—1 down before I got going!' Really, there is no excuse for this situation ever arising.

The best way to avoid feeling stiff and cold is to get into the habit of warming-up before a game. Some people feel inhibited about exercising, particularly in front of spectators and opponents. However, if players are encouraged to get into the routine of warming-up early in their playing careers this should not be the case.

I generally find a quiet corner away from the public gaze just before I am

Four types of stretching exercises.

Bounding exercise.

due on the table, and then go through a series of stretching and loosening exercises. Warming-up is a great way to avoid pulling muscles and sustaining unnecessary injury.

It should be used before a coaching session. A suitable warm-up in this case should comprise about 60 per cent jogging, skipping, running backwards, short sprints and so on, and 40 per cent loosening and stretching exercises.

Fitness fads

We now live in an age of body consciousness. Fitness and health is big business and slimming has become an industry in itself.

While many fitness fads can do everything except get you fit, there has been one recent trend that I have adopted and which has become a firm favourite with a lot of the other England girls — pop mobility. Exercising to music is a great way to train, relieving as it does the boredom and monotony of keeping in shape, and I wholeheartedly recommend it.

Obviously, being overweight does nothing to improve your game, but like any sportsman or sportswoman you need to eat properly. Eat less, yes, but physical activity means you need food that meets the calorific (energy) demands of playing table tennis, and preferably foods that are high in protein and low in fat. If you are playing in a tournament, breakfast is an important meal because when you have just woken up your blood sugar will be low. Skipping breakfast can lead to eating snacks later on in the day. Bacon and eggs are out, but muesli cereal and dried fruit is light enough and probably higher in energy value. I am not an advocate of vitamin supplements, but in hot, humid climates salt tablets can be a great help.

Finally, there is nothing like feeling fit for giving you a mental lift. Being in good condition should help your confidence for serious competition. This in turn must make a difference to your chances of winning.

9 The role of the coach

In modern table tennis, the coach is someone who wears many different hats — manager, mentor and motivator, psychologist and physiologist, teacher and trainer, diplomat and van driver. The coach can be many things, but above all his main aim should be to raise the general standard of performance at all levels and to encourage the talented player to reach his or her full potential. It may well be that in fulfilling this aim, the coach must act in some or all of the parts listed above.

For someone coaching at a grass-roots level and involved with the same group of players, the role of the coach changes according to how the players develop. Perhaps the best way to look at the coach's involvement in this development is to take a hypothetical situation in which a complete novice progresses through to international standard. We will assume for this example that the same coach sticks by the player throughout.

The beginner

At this stage the coach is the teacher and demonstrator, showing how the four basic shots are played and 'grooving in' a sound technique. There is little involvement in competition, so tactics and match play are not important. Simple things like explaining the rules of the game, how to serve correctly and which bat to use are all instances where the coach's knowledge and experience are important.

Two to three years

By now, our protegé is beginning to master the more advanced shots. The coach might not be a sufficiently good player to practise with, and it is important that he is aware of his own limitations in this department. Better players are brought in to practise with, and the coach begins to adopt more of a background role but still ironing out faults as and when they emerge. The player is probably competing in the local league and entering the occasional tournament. It is for the coach to encourage the correct approach to the game, ensuring that the player gets into the habit of

The author, pictured with some of England's up-and-coming girl players and E.T.T.A. Chairman, Tom Blunn.

warming-up properly. Respect for the umpire and for the opposition, along with good table manners, are qualities which the coach should instil in the player.

At this stage in competition, winning is not always important. It is a period where basic experience is acquired. If the player is beaten simply because the opponent has intelligently exploited a fundamental weakness, then the coach should be able to spot this and work on the deficiency.

Three to four years

By now a style of play should be emerging, and it is important that the coach should appreciate this and be aware of the player's natural inclinations. We must be wary of producing stereotyped players. All the top players are stylists of one form or another, and I cannot help but feel that the age of the all-rounder is finished.

The coach's role as a teacher of stroke play has almost totally disappeared. Now it is motivation that is important — ensuring effort and application in the player and an attitude of playing to win, and not playing 'not to lose'. There is a subtle difference — the former is the positive way, while playing not to lose can mean that the coach simply has a retriever on his hands. In the long run this will not be good enough to get the player to the top. The coach is now almost exclusively involved with the player as a competitor — he is teaching him or her how to compete effectively.

Six to seven years

By now, the player is representing the county and is pushing up the national ranking list, perhaps vying for a place in the national squad.

The player should be correctly aroused for a match, not too nervous and not too confident. For the purposes of this discussion we have assumed the same player/coach relationship throughout and, as you know, this is very rare. The player will usually have many coaches, as I have in my playing career. It is for the coach to spend a long time getting to know the player's personality and mind. On England Junior Training Camps, I spend days getting to know the players. This is important because it can sometimes be dangerous if you misjudge a player's character. For example, it may appear at first sight that a player is too relaxed, when in fact the opposite may be the case and the condition is one of extreme anxiety. To say 'this match is vital' could be disastrous. More appropriate would be words of encouragement, along the lines of 'you've nothing to lose, so do your best'.

Tactics are now an important factor, and the coach must be able to examine the opponent's game and discuss this with the player. In particular, attention should be given to the service and receive, which services are the most suitable and where and how best to return the ball.

There is always a danger, however, that players can become too reliant on the coach for advice, so it is no good if they are always turning during a match to the coach seeking inspiration. You never see Desmond Douglas or myself doing that. While on the table it is for the players to get themselves out of difficult situations. The coach, then, should beware of mentally dependent players.

There should always be encouragement when they have lost, assuming of course there has been a 100 per cent effort. Discussions on what went wrong can usually wait until emotions have returned to normal. Only in very rare instances would I reprimand a player after a match, and this is solely when they have not really tried.

By now our player is quite a celebrity, with all the attendant pressures of being a top-class athlete. It is for the coach to see that it stays that way, by helping to deflect all these outside influences. The coach's role is now one of allowing the player to concentrate entirely on the game ahead. Officials, sponsors, press and photographers are dealt with by the coach, who now

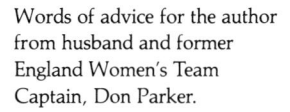

Words of advice for the author from husband and former England Women's Team Captain, Don Parker.

A smirk of success on winning the 1980 Top Twelve in Hungary.

plays the part of manager and diplomat, taking any unnecessary pressures off the players.

At the end of the day a well-balanced, mature individual should emerge, both a promising table-tennis player and a sociable person. The coach should not have been party to breeding a table-tennis moron who knows the game and nothing else. The player's development should leave ample room for schoolwork or work and other interests. After all, very few players actually make it to the top, so there has to be something for them to fall back on.

In conclusion

Coaching is a vast subject and could make a book in itself. Unfortunately, in this small chapter we cannot explore every argument and angle in detail. The English Table Tennis Association runs a first-class coaching awards scheme, and anyone who fancies their chances in this field of the game only has to get in touch with them for further details.

However, you might want to consider these final few points before you do so. Do not go into it thinking that coaching will become a vehicle for your own aspirations or desire for prestige and fame. By their very nature, coaches are secondary to the player, as the critic is to the artist, and that is how it should be. Unlike football, coaches are fairly anonymous — albeit important figures. So, please do not think you can become a Brian Clough.

Coaching is not exclusively about finding world-beaters, but about raising the general standard throughout the game. A lot of coaches I have come across are very wary of releasing their players to work with other coaches. What they are doing is stifling the players' development by preventing them benefiting from different practices or new approaches. Two heads are better than one, so try not to hold the players back — be prepared to see them go their own way, hopefully to the top. They will remember you if they are good enough to get there.

10 Combination bat—myth or magic?

The phenomenon of the combination bat

In 1980, at the European Championships at Berne in Switzerland, something astonishing happened that had enormous implications for the future of table tennis. John Hilton, an insurance salesman from Manchester, made monkeys out of the best players in Europe and stole the men's title from right under their noses. As the press were quick to point out, he managed to do this with a 'magic bat'.

Not that this 'magic bat' was anything really new. As long ago as the early 1960s, a gentleman called Xhang Xie Lin in China was experimenting very successfully with what he called the 'Yin-Yan' bat. His countrymen were not slow in dubbing him 'the magician'; it is strange how table tennis attracts these mystical adjectives.

The 'Yin-Yan' bat — positive/negative, or male/female, if you want a rough translation — is essentially what we now know as the combination bat. There was no real magic about John's or Mr Xhang's bat; each was simply a bat whose two sides were covered with different kinds of rubber, having quite different properties and so quite opposite effects on the ball. But this was not the sole reason for John's success. What the press overlooked was the way John *used* this particular device. He twiddled it in his hand, effectively giving him two versions of each shot, and he attacked and feigned topspin with the 'dead' anti-topspin side. He played an all-round game which no one else had previously thought of, or fully exploited.

Nevertheless, the combination bat has caused a controversy in the game. Its critics claim it gives poor players an unfair advantage; others say it is ruining table tennis as a spectator sport and should be banned. Its supporters, on the other hand, will tell you that it is immensely difficult to master, and anyway, many players can now read the combination-bat game. Its impact, they say, is on the decline.

Before we look at these points in more detail and before I discuss my own recent decision to use the combination bat, we should first look in some depth at the technical aspects. What types of combination bat are available; what the bat can do; how to play with it and how to play against

England's John Hilton — the table-tennis success story of 1980.

it are all points that need looking at before any objective discussion of the ethics can be really informed.

What is a combination bat?

The most popular and effective combination bats have a conventional reversed rubber on one side combined with either a long-pimpled rubber or a 'dead' anti-loop type rubber of the same colour on the other. The effect of both these bats is to produce different spins with the same stroke, depending upon which side of the bat is used.

The properties of reversed rubber should be familiar by now; chopping the ball produces backspin, looping produces topspin. Reversed rubber imparts spin, but anti-loop and long pimples do not share this quality and are what might be termed 'parasite' rubbers. They feed off the spin that is already on the ball that is about to be played.

Long-pimpled rubber is a comparatively recent introduction to the modern game. Pimpled rubber is nothing new — it has been around for years — but the long, soft-pimpled type is a refinement. Depending on the nature of the sponge layer beneath it, it has bounce and speed or a high recoil coefficient for the more technically minded. However, in its faster varieties it is a difficult rubber to control. Because the pimples are soft, though, it offers little or no resistance to spin. Therefore a topspin ball that is blocked with long pimples will return with a small amount of chop on it. The ball continues to spin in the same direction because the pimples allow this to happen, as the diagram shows. Of course, if the same shot were

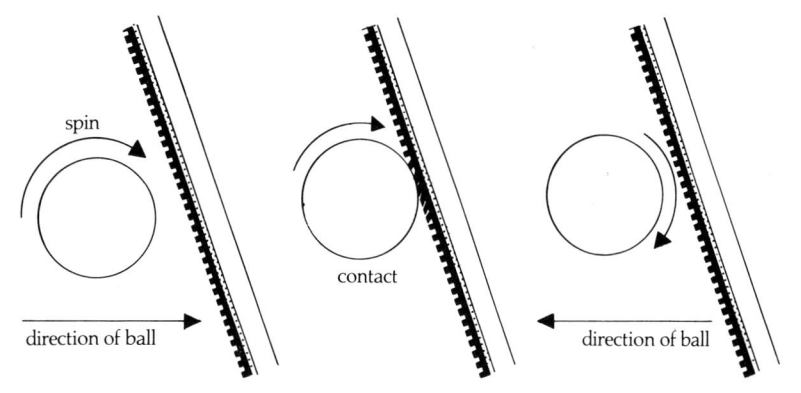

The soft pimples bend at the point of contact and offer little resistance to the spin already on the ball. As a result the ball returns with 'chop' on it.

performed with orthodox reverse rubber, the ball would return with a marginal amount of topspin on it.

Because of its inherent speed characteristic it is a useful rubber for top-spinning with, but only if the ball to be played has heavy chop on it. As I said before, it is a parasitic rubber; it cannot really *impart* much spin, but it does have the ability to accentuate the spin already on the ball. To complicate matters further, some manufacturers are now producing this already strange animal with pimples cut to an angle. This serves to heighten the effects already mentioned.

Anti-loop or anti-spin rubber is a smooth and very dead rubber. It first emerged into the international arena at the World Championships in Nagoya, Japan, in 1971. A gentleman from France called Jean-Paul Weber enjoyed some minor success with a bat made up entirely of anti-loop rubber. Although it is much slower than long pimples, it is easier to control and allows a far greater margin of error. It has little resistance to spin (though not to the same degree as long pimples), so it is possible to achieve a similar effect when blocking topspin. Because the essence of the combination-bat game is twiddling the bat in the hand and being able to use the anti-spin surface on both wings, anti-loop is more suitable for this deception because of its high control factor.

Playing against it — a science?

Playing both with and against the combination bat has become a whole new game in itself. Because of its low resistance to spin, orthodox

10. Combination bat — myth or magic?

principles, such as watching your opponent's bat angle and racket speed, go right out of the window; this is further compounded by the 'twiddling' technique. Studying how to read spin has become quite a science.

The first priority should be to try actually to make out which side of the bat is being used. This is difficult on receiving service and the third ball, as many combination-bat players insist on keeping the bat out of view or under the table on every possible occasion. Obviously, pimples are more easily distiguished than anti-loop, though in the right lighting situations even anti-loop can sometimes be picked out because of its dull matt appearance.

One of the best ways to read spin, which is reliable irrespective of the conditions, is actually to look at the markings on the ball. If you can see the markings, then the ball is not spinning. In the team event of the 1980 European Championships in Berne when England played Sweden, John Hilton was on the table against Ulf Thorsell in a crucial game. Thorsell 'accidentally' stood on the ball simply so that he could have a new one with much clearer markings. Not that the orthodox player can take much heart from this occasion, though; Thorsell still lost.

The third method is to try and listen to the sound of the ball as it hits the bat. Top players can detect which side has been used with their backs to the table. But the combination-bat player has adapted to remove this clue by stamping his feet as contact is made with the ball. The Chinese, of course, are undaunted and I have been told of one of their players who, with his back to the table, can *still* identify which side has been used on service — by judging the time between the bounces. The timespan varies by fractions of a second, according to whether or not there is any spin on the ball.

If all else fails, watch the flight of the ball; true topspin causes the ball to dip in flight while true backspin makes it lift. Fake versions, as played by the anti-loop or pimples, should not show the same characteristics, as the diagram illustrates.

Left: with topspin on the ball, angle *a* is greater than angle *b*.
Right: with chop on the ball, angle *a* is smaller than angle *b*.

topspin   chop

Istvan Jonyer of Hungary recently changed to a combination bat. This may appear at first sight to be a surprising move for someone like Jonyer, who is one of the top exponents of the powerful topspin game. However, this deceptive bat has given his game a new dimension, a revival even.

When Hungary played Czechoslovakia in the team event of the 1982 European Championships, Jonyer efficiently despatched both Orlowski and Dvoracek. His next game was against Jindrich Pansky, who usually plays very well against the combination bat. Aware of Pansky's skill in this area, Jonyer discreetly changed bats for this contest and used an orthodox bat with reverse rubber on both sides. It was only when the game was nearly lost that Pansky realised that he had been tricked. A very basic error on Pansky's behalf, perhaps, but nonetheless a tale with a moral.

That moral relates to the rules which permit players to inspect one another's bats prior to the start of play — a facility which Pansky would have done better to take advantage of.

Playing with the combination bat

There are now a lot of young, talented combination-bat players around in England, the most notable two being Carl Prean and Billy Gleave, both still juniors at the time of writing. Of course, the English national penchant for imitation is rife once more and many youngsters have been inspired to follow these two fine examples. Because of international success by combination-bat players, rubber manufacturers are not far behind in fuelling the craze.

England's Carl Prean — awkward, unorthodox but an exceptionally talented young player.

To play well with a combination bat — and I stress the word 'well' — is not an easy task. All too often I see players changing to a combination bat for the wrong reason — namely, to cover up a basic weakness or flaw in their game. It should be used to enhance what is a sound game in the first place. Youngsters starting with such a bat very early in their careers should pay particular attention to the basic strokes and work *extra* hard at developing them in every area. They should also learn to twiddle, and to be able to play all the basic strokes with both sides of the bat to gain a quick understanding of the properties of the rubbers involved. Because this type of game revolves around the art of deception, the bat should be kept out of sight prior to serving and when receiving service.

Initially, young players find that points come quick and easy. But that is only when they play amongst their own age group, who are also at an early stage of development and cannot read the spin. Coaches and parents should be thinking long-term and ensuring that their protegés have a strong, efficient game when they mature.

A combination bat is at its most effective on the service and receive, and during a push rally close to the table when the difference between the spin generated by either side is at its most extreme. Even as a defender, I set out to attack the third ball with the reverse rubber, hopefully having initially deceived my opponent with a serve using the anti-loop. It is in the service/receive area of the game that good use of this type of racket can be lethal.

For the defensive combination-bat player, it is also important to be able to both chop and float with the reverse rubber. To be forced away from the table, and to defend almost exclusively with the anti-loop because of its high control factor, is to sacrifice the bat's inherent advantage of deception. For the attacking player it is equally important that any pushed ball is hit with the reverse side. To do this with the long pimples or anti-loop sets the ball up and gives an open invitation to the opponent to attack. Conversely, the topspin ball should be hit or blocked with the anti-spin side.

In the last European Championships at Budapest, I managed to go unbeaten in the team event, beating even the eventual ladies champion Bettine Vriesekoop of Holland. My form continued to hold good in the singles event, where I played Bettine again in the final. But here I fell right into one of the pitfalls I have just been highlighting. I hit too many of her pushed balls with the anti-loop and instead of misreading it, as in our previous encounter, she took one pace back and, taking advantage of its slow pace, viciously topspun the ball to the wings. This put me out of position and gave her the edge and of course the title.

Looking back on that occasion and on the development of the combination bat in the international arena, I would advise the prospective

Bettine Vriesekoop of Holland, the 1982 European Ladies' Singles Champion.

combination-bat player to opt for anti-loop in preference to long pimples. I have played with both. From late 1978 to early 1982, I used long pimples on one side and enjoyed enormous success on the domestic front, and initially on the international circuit. But abroad I found that the heavy chop I could get from the pimples against the topspin ball was being dealt with comfortably by the foreign attacking players, who could quite easily topspin the ball over the net. As a result I was finding myself under a lot of pressure during games, and the difficulty in controlling the ball with long pimples was not helping. So in January 1982 I switched to anti-loop; it gives me more margin of error and it is not as easy for the opposition to see as pimples are.

John Hilton — an objective analysis

As I pointed out at the beginning of this chapter, John Hilton's 1980 European Championship success was largely reported in the press as something of a freak. A large part of the table-tennis establishment saw it in similar terms, as a one-off that he could never really hope to live up to.

I believe that these assumptions were unfounded. I trained with John Hilton at the two-week England Training Camp, held shortly before the Championships. This was the first time he had been able to attend a full two-week camp because of his natural commitment to a full-time job outside the game. During the time at the Camp he utilised his time to maximum possible effect; he trained exceptionally hard, he practised diligently and applied himself completely to the build-up for the big event.

At the event itself he played at his peak both in the team event and obviously in the single event. His preparation had brought him to a stage where he played to the very best of his ability, as history now shows.

The English attitude to John Hilton is a distorted one. Domestically he is very much a known quantity and most of our top players are completely familiar with his game. Therefore, we had a ridiculous situation in which he was ranked one in Europe, two in England and three at Manchester YMCA! However, in Europe and internationally he is a genuine innovator — the first player really to think of attacking with anti-loop, the inventor of the anti-loop or fake topspin. He is the best exponent of this type of game, which has taken him years to perfect.

His success in the 1980 European Championships was the culmination of a subtle, subversive assault on the international circuit. Previously he had always been respected overseas, as his success in the team event of the 1978 European Championships at Duisberg shows. It is not possible to beat the likes of Dvoracek, Secretin and Gergely as soundly as he did, through trickery alone. The reason why he does not now continue to enjoy the same success is purely because those same players have become familiar with his game through many subsequent encounters. This is exactly in the same way as our top players are familiar with him. Indeed, this familiarity at home may have been the key to his success, as it tuned his game to perfection before his attack on a largely unsuspecting Europe.

Naturally John's game revolves around a skilful, calculated expertise with his combination bat. John looks after his bat better than many people look after their cars, much to the amusement of his England colleagues. Before a game he carefully washes the anti-loop rubber, and then vigorously rubs it with a towel to the point where he is actually polishing it. This is to get it as smooth as possible, in much the same way as a cricketer polishes the ball before bowling. He then dries it with a hairdryer. This heats up the rubber and gives him that extra bit of pace when using it to attack.

John has worked terrifically hard for his success and he deserves every lasting moment. I wish him well and hope it continues for him.

The ethical questions

From what I have said about John, coupled with my own decision to use this new type of bat, it may sound as though I am in favour of it. This is not the case. I strongly feel that the rules relating to bats should be altered, not necessarily to ban the combination bat altogether but at least to remove some of its more deceptive qualities. Why then, you may ask, do I hypocritically play with one if I feel this way? Unfortunately, it is not that simple.

Table tennis has been my life and I owe nearly everything I have to it; it is my job, my way of earning a decent living. A woman in this game has to be at the top to make any money, and even then it pales into insignificance alongside the earnings of a leading women's tennis professional.

The author in action for her country.

10. Combination bat — myth or magic?

When I saw the Chinese at Birmingham in 1977 with these 'new' bats demoralising everyone, I was initially appalled and was convinced that this bat was killing the game, particularly for spectators. When later I was getting poor results at the hands of these players, my convictions about the immorality of it had to be put to one side. Losing to Judit Magos of Hungary in the 1978 European Final was the last straw. I would have been stupid, as a professional sportswoman, not to have opted for the combination bat. Everything about my game was entirely suited to it, and my results improved, among them a number of wins over Magos. In short, it

Judit Magos of Hungary, one of a handful of Western players to master the penhold grip.

was a case of adapt or die; and for the time being, at least, the ethics of this issue are quite separate from my career as a professional table-tennis player.

It is interesting to note that John also favours some sort of legislation to limit the combination bat. The English Table Tennis Association at the last I.T.T.F. meeting on this very question voted in favour of an amendment to the rules, which was not in their interest as we have an obvious wealth of good players who use it. Like myself and John, our concern is for the long-term effect that it will have on the game as a spectator sport. The best game to watch is one of attacker versus defender with exciting long rallies and gasps of amazement from the assembled masses. The 1948 World Championships in London attracted over ten thousand spectators, with tickets sold out three to four months in advance. It was one of the most popular post-war sports simply because it was a compelling spectacle when practised by the greats. This is not true today.

Watching a game of table tennis between two combination-bat players is like watching fencing — meaningless, unless you are a player yourself. Only then can you understand why they look so amateurish when they misread the spin. The game will only survive if it remains a good spectator sport. If it is a good game to watch, then new talent will be attracted to it.

There is no doubt that in the combination-bat game there are factors affecting the end result which have nothing to do with skill. Earlier in this chapter I discussed the difficulty involved in distinguishing which side of the bat has hit the ball. One of the more popular techniques is to listen to the sound, but this is not possible in a noisy hall.

A typical incident which highlights this point happened when I played Judit Magos in Budapest at the 1982 European Championships. At the same time as we were due to play, three of her fellow countrymen, Jonyer, Klampar and Gergely were involved in quarter-final matches on adjoining tables. The very noisy home crowd would make it impossible for her to listen to the sound of the ball on my bat. Accordingly, her coach came over to the England bench seeking an adjournment until the noise died down. My captain, Nicky Jarvis, refused this concession. When the neighbouring games finished, relative quiet settled on our contest and she could now hear. The advice I then received from the England bench was to stamp at the point of contact, to disguise the sound. I won — but it was not truly table tennis. At the time, I did not question the morality of stamping, for reasons I have already explained. But the game cannot go on like this.

Some players and coaches will argue that the colour of a piece of rubber should not affect a player's ability to win, but I disagree. Engelbert Huging, the West German defender, claimed in a heated argument that he would play just as successfully with two completely different coloured rubbers on his bat. In an attempt to prove his point, he used just such a bat, but he soon found that he was nowhere near as successful, and he quickly reverted to rubbers of the same colour. Indeed, a number of combination-bat players are now practising with different coloured sides in an attempt to anticipate the outcome of the next I.T.T.F. meeting on the subject.

Undoubtedly, the combination bat has presented all the world ruling bodies with a sizable problem that needs resolving quickly. The introduction of sponge rubber, the prototype of reverse, caused a similar controversy in the early 1950s. Then, it was an innocuous little Japanese gentleman named Satoh who had Bergmann and Barna in a spin, if you will excuse the terrible pun, by using rubber inches thick!

The I.T.T.F. were swift in legislating to limit the thickness of the rubber to the present-day maximum of 4 mm. Most players at that time were hard-bat defenders, and the sponge bat swept through them like a flaming sword. We reached a pitch in the early 1970s where defenders, particularly in the men's game, were very much in a minority. Reversed sponge rubber has been developed within its legal limits to a point where enormous spin and speed can be generated, which obviously favours the attacking players.

If the combination-bat rules are to be changed to force the use of different-coloured rubbers, then it is only fair that the power of the attacking player should be further limited by reducing the maximum thickness allowed, to 3.5 mm. I would even go so far as to suggest a complete standardisation of the bat's minimal thickness of rubber, so that pure skill becomes the deciding factor.

11 Ball in the mind?

Table tennis psychology — the right mental approach

The problem with a subject like this is to know where to begin, because it is such a vast area for discussion. Nevertheless, I will be brave and make a start by simply defining what 'the mental approach' is, as I see it. It is the psychological arousal of the player to produce an attitude of mind which in turn will enable him or her to give the best performance.

To try to be as comprehensive as possible, I will look at how this can be achieved from four different angles — the player away from table tennis; the player in practice and training; the player prior to a match; and finally, the player in actual competition.

This chapter is closely linked with chapter 9, 'The role of the coach', because much of what I have to say directly and indirectly concerns the coach's relationship with the player. Not for one minute, though, do I consider this to be the complete and definitive picture. Indeed, I would hope that many of the issues I raise will become points for further thought and discussion among readers.

The player away from table tennis

As with any other game, the need for sleep and relaxation is just as important as the need to practise. It is not just a question of simply not playing, but of being able to extract yourself mentally from the game. When you do come to play or practise you will then be fresh and enthusiastic, not stale and overworked.

I like to relax by taking part in other sports, in particular tennis and squash, which I find are beneficial to my game simply because they are 'bat—ball' games. They have what physiologists term a 'positive transfer value', when played in moderation. I avoid games like hockey, not because I do not care for it but because I could easily get injured.

Young players need the watchful eye of their parents to ensure they do not overdo things. This is a tricky subject, because parents can become — quite understandably — emotionally involved in their child's playing career. Ideally, a parent should be the financier and transport manager and should leave the coaching to the coach. Unfortunately, some parents can become so involved that their children are nothing more than an extension of themselves. I have had the misfortune to come across instances where a parent has actually hit his child for losing because he has become so wrapped up in the game himself. This is a very unhealthy state of affairs and does little to support or encourage a young mind. Of course, I must then quickly point out the many successful parent-child relationships in this field — there is, as usual, no absolute golden rule in these matters.

Sometimes too much playing can do more harm than good. At the end of a season, I want nothing more than to get away from the game completely for a few weeks, and I do not consider this to be a bad thing. After all, when the new season starts you cannot afford to be fed up with your game.

So when you are not playing or practising, try to forget table tennis completely. Try not to worry about whom you are due to play in the next match, or whether or not you will be picked for the team. These are typical preoccupations of a mentally weak player.

Just put table tennis out of your mind.

The England team pictured before a 1981 European League fixture. Clockwise from left to right — Linda Jarvis, Paul Day, Desmond Douglas, John Hilton, Peter Simpson (non-playing captain) and, in the car, the author.

The player in practice and training

It stands to reason that if you concentrate hard when practising, then there is bound to be an improvement in your application to a match.

Of course, this is easier said than done and requires much from the coach, the nature of the practice session and the quality of fellow-players in the group. Generally speaking the best player benefits the least in group practice, whereas the worst player will benefit the most. But practice routines can be set up which will exert the better player, even though his opponent is of a lesser standard. The coach should be aware of the differing abilities of the group and should take this into account.

Group practice situations are reciprocal in nature; when you are acting as the controller in a particular routine, do your best to help your colleague at the other end of the table and try not to be selfish. The quality of the controlled ball governs the value that your partner will get out of practising. Equally, the coach should be aware of when to break the practice and let the players rest, so that maximum value is gained. For example, fast looping from various points can only be properly maintained for ten minutes or so because it is so physically demanding.

The physical demands of the game can be fairly easily recreated in practice and through training. What cannot be reproduced, though, are the psychological effects of game conditions. How do you recreate the pressure a player may experience at 20—20 in the third, with hundreds of people watching? Obviously, it is impossible. This can only be gained properly through experience, though there are techniques which can improve your resistance to this sort of pressure.

One sometimes used in the England training camps is 'autogenic training', in which the player is in a state of 'relaxed concentration'. It is introduced in a practice session before the members of the group play a few games against one another.

What happens is that the players lie on the floor and concentrate for three minutes on silence, peace and quiet. They then go and play. At the next session this is repeated but is followed by a further three minutes where the topic of concentration is 'feeling warm'. The players then return to the tables to play. At the next session, the same routine is repeated, but a third period of three minutes is added where the subject for concentration is 'feeling heavy'.

These three cycles are repeated in subsequent sessions. What should happen is that the body becomes conditioned by the mind into lapsing into a state of extreme relaxation as soon as it hits the floor. Once this reaction sets in automatically and the player no longer needs a subject for concentration, the theory is that the mind will be free to concentrate on the game ahead. Hopefully, if used before a match, a state of optimum arousal is reached.

Another popular method of psychological conditioning is desensitisation training. This also involves the player lying down, in comfortable surroundings so as to relax the body completely. Once this pleasant state of relaxation is attained, the mind then compiles a list of all those fears which worry the player. It might be the choice of ball at a forthcoming tournament, an opponent's particular style, combination bats or certain services that are hard to return. By concentrating on each fear in turn while in a state of complete relaxation, the hope is that the fear in question will be diminished and the player will become desensitised to the effect it has on his/her game. The theory is that the mind will subconsciously associate the particular fear with feeling relaxed. When the game begins, the impact of the fear should be nowhere near as strong.

In an attempt to improve someone's competitive nature, the coach could ensure that he or she plays more games in practice, rather than simply reproducing strokes within practice routines. To add more tension to practice match play, some of the Europeans gamble against one another — though I will not court controversy by endorsing this habit.

The further I have come in the game, the less enjoyable training and practice have become; some of my colleagues in the England squad also find this. Players must recognise that there are only so many things that can be done with two bats, a ball and a table! You will therefore need a high degree of self-motivation if practice is to be of any benefit at higher standards.

With this in mind you might want to consider the time of day you practice. Most tournaments are day-long events; some players do well in the morning but will flag in the afternoon, others are the opposite. Try to schedule your practice for those times of the day when your competitive performances are particularly weak.

The player prior to a match

It is at this point that being fully aroused becomes very important. As I have explained, it depends to a large extent on the nature and disposition of the individual as to how this is achieved. Everyone, though, should try to avoid things which might unsettle them before a competition at any level.

For example, if you are going to a match or tournament, make sure you have all the right equipment and that you will look the part. If you look and feel good, this will increase your chances of putting in a good performance. Make sure you have a spare bat and spare clothing if necessary. I remember one instance where the former World Champion,

The player prior to a match

Mitsuru Kohno of Japan, had to withdraw from an important event because he forgot his glasses, and had no spare pair. A simple error, perhaps, but nevertheless a very costly one.

At one time some of the England Juniors would admit defeat before they even got on the table. If the opposition happened to be Czechoslovakia or Sweden, they seemed resigned to defeat. But now they are enjoying some measure of success in Europe, and the confidence of players like Carl Prean, Billy Gleave and Lisa Bellinger is rubbing off on other members. One wonders how much benefit China gains simply from being China and feared by other nations. The lesson is obvious — a little confidence will go a long way, and could mean the difference between winning and losing.

Playing conditions and lighting might not necessarily be quite what you expected. Try not to let this affect you; after all, they are the same for both players. If possible get to the venue early, have a good knock and familiarise yourself with the environment.

Before the game, try and sit down with your coach and discuss your opponent from a tactical point of view — what sort of serves you

England's Lisa Bellinger — one of the brightest prospects for years.

anticipate will be the most effective, how best to receive service, and so on. Analyse your opponent's game, and look for areas in it that may be weak and could be exploited.

One of the most valuable pieces of equipment I have in my kit is a notebook. This contains my recollections and analysis of previous opponents I have met. It has become a very useful aide-memoire, particularly if you play a lot of tournaments and take part in one or two leagues. It is not always easy to recall whom you have played in the past, particularly in my case because at international level I have had to play against thousands of opponents.

It is worthwhile considering how you might spend the fifteen minutes or so before you go on the table. Some players relax and compose themselves by chatting to their colleagues, others like to disappear to a quiet area of the room to be alone. Again, it is what suits each individual best. Myself, I prefer to be alone, and I usually find that my pre-match warm-up is the best time to prepare and compose myself.

The player in competition

Go into your game in a positive frame of mind, highly motivated and wanting to win. Going on to the table with the attitude that you will just keep the ball going might not be enough. Your mind must now be closed to all other distractions.

Concentration and determination are prerequisites of success.

I have seen some players get upset even before the first point is played because they have allowed themselves to be distracted by trivial occurrences. One of the most famous instances that springs to mind happened during the 1980 European Championships at Berne in Switzerland. The stadium was enormous, so large in fact that a breeze built up travelling from one side to the other. This meant that one side of the table was a better side to be at than the other, because of the strange effect it was having on the flight of the ball.

John Hilton faced a difficult opponent in the early rounds and lost the toss. The umpire turned his back on the players and went back to his seat. His opponent grasped the ball ready to serve — whereupon John moved to the better side of the table. This was quite within his rights, believing as he did that his opponent had elected to serve.

Unfortunately, with his back turned at the time, the umpire missed what was going on. Taking advantage of this fact, his opponent then appeared to reject the serve, preferring the better end instead. To the umpire, ignorant of what had happened, John seemed to be protesting unfairly; after all, everything seemed in order.

John was very upset at having been cheated and this encounter proved to be the most difficult on his route to the 1980 Men's Title. However, he had learned his lesson by the time the final came along. The opponent here was Josef Dvoracek of Czechoslovakia who, prior to the start of play, firmly indicated his preferences by placing his bat on the better side of the table. The umpire promptly returned it to him, explaining that the choice of ends depended on the outcome of the toss. Nonetheless, Dvoracek still won the toss.

Throughout this, John sat calmly and appeared totally above what was going on. It did not seem to matter what side he was to play from. Bemused by John's seemingly total indifference, Dvoracek indicated firmly to the umpire that he would serve. Once this had been noted, John strode to the other side of the table, exercising his right to the choice of end. In his eagerness, Dvoracek had duped himself. You could see the look of despair on his face. The rest is history and the lesson is clear — you need strength of character and firm self-control, so that little things will not upset you.

Once the game has started, the important thing to remember is to play the point. Try not to think too much about the score or the fact that you might be one game down; this will only distract you from the real task in hand. Once a point is lost, or won even, forget it and concentrate on the next one. With rallies lasting on average three to four seconds, each point is an explosion of concentration.

At 15−5 up, the game can still be lost. Relax only when you get to 21. It is amazing how the score does affect some people's level of concentra-

11. Ball in the mind?

tion. Frequently, I have seen situations where from 5—15 down players level the game at 17-all. What invariably happens next is that they relax, thinking that their task is complete. Their opponent then takes advantage of their relaxation to sneak home as winner.

Twenty-all in the third game also throws up a valuable insight into the character of a player. Of course, it is a high-pressure situation and there are players who seem to enjoy it, winning more than they lose. Some freeze completely; others are so determined not to freeze that they go for outrageous shots that are simply not playable.

Tears of joy on becoming 1976 European Champion.

As a defender, I have often been involved in expedite situations in the game. The reason why many people seem to lose expedite games is because they panic. It is useful to consider how long twelve strokes really is. In fact, it is an unusually long time. If I happen to be serving, where the onus is on me to win the point, then I will look toward attacking on the third ball. If I cannot win the point, then I will relax and wait until the ninth or tenth ball to try and finish the point. Above all, you must not panic.

On the other hand, if I am the receiver, then I will try to tempt my opponent with the floated ball, putting pressure on them to finish the point and hopefully snatch their shot and make a mistake.

Though it does not occur often, except in the international circuit, matches can be played over the best of five games. If this is the case, you must condition yourself not to relax after winning two games, which over the best of three would obviously make you the winner.

Perhaps a classic case of this was in the 1982 European Championships in Budapest. England's Desmond Douglas romped away to two games up against the young Swede, Jan Ove Waldner. However, he lost the next three because he failed to maintain the same sort of pressure.

Some things, such as your opponent's good luck, are out of your control. All the same, do not let it affect you. Many players get irritated over net balls, but this is quite unnecessary when you actually take the time to examine the net-ball issue.

Ignoring the fact that your opponent has to cope with your net balls, I reckon only 50 per cent of those that you have to deal with are irretrievable. There are then about 25 per cent that you can get back and a remaining 25 per cent you can even turn to your advantage. All in all, then, you come out on top.

There are occasionally moments in the game when the umpire makes a

The author, pictured with Mrs Nancy Evans, General Secretary of the E.T.T.A.

11. Ball in the mind?

The author being presented with the trophy for becoming the 1976 European Champion.

decision you might not agree with. Question it by all means, but do not argue. If the umpire stands firm, forget it. It was only one point, after all, and not the game. Settle down and prepare yourself for the next point.

This question of umpires' decisions brings me neatly on to the controversial issue of 'table manners'. The very last thing I would want to see is for table tennis to turn into a sport populated by some of the more 'colourful' characters that we see in tennis. No one should ever be allowed to become bigger than the game. Our national association should watch out for this and avoid getting itself into a situation where it becomes compromised. We need talented players — but not talented players who behave like prima-donnas. Everyone is expendable, and if they cannot act in the interests of the game it does not matter how good they are.

Indeed, if swearing ever becomes an acceptable part of the game, then this will see the end of my involvement at every possible level.

Control of emotion is a factor which is within your power, and one that can even be turned to your advantage. It will be decisive in how you cope with an opponent who insists on going for his towel between every point. If he sees that it annoys you, he will do it even more. Likewise, if you express disappointment or emotion at losing points then this will only help your opponent. At the end of the day you can only do your best.

Defeat is never easy to swallow, but shake hands all the same and congratulate your opponent as you would if you had been the winner. It is also good manners to shake hands and thank the umpire. The crowd will always warm to the valiant loser. There will be another time, and you must think that the result will then be turned in your favour. Try not to look for excuses for your defeat, and above all do not blame your coach. This will only mean that you are mentally dependent. Losing, in younger players, can be therapeutic. It can teach them a lot about themselves and, of course, they are at an age when areas of their game can be improved.

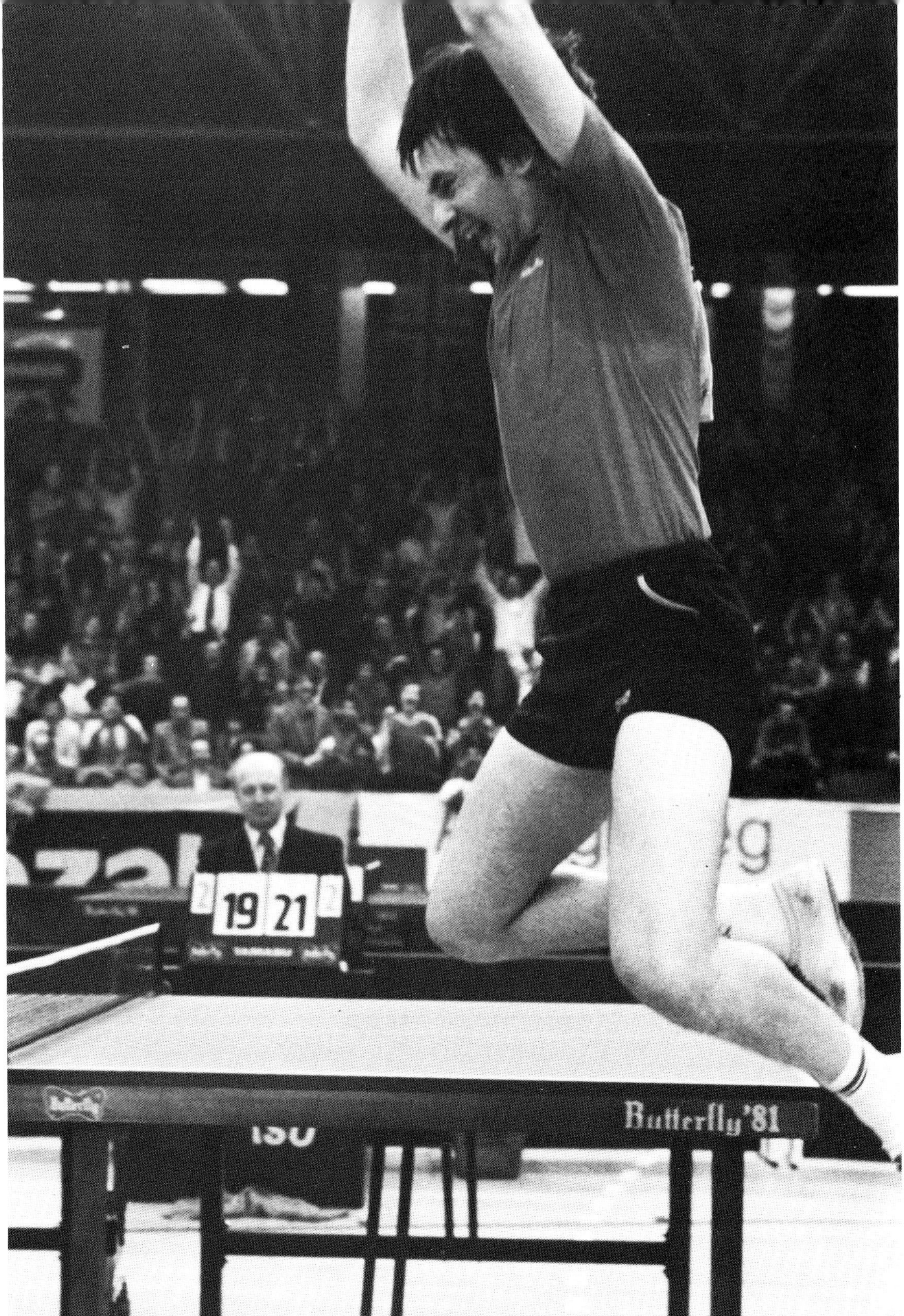

19 21
Butterfly '81

12 Winning tactics

Which comes first, the right tactics or the right mental approach? It is something of a chicken and egg situation, because both concepts are inextricably linked. On balance, though, I feel that tactics are of no use whatsoever if the player in question is not properly mentally prepared. This is why I have left the question of tactics until the psychological aspects of the game have been fully explored.

To be successful in any sport, whether it be in a one-to-one situation or in a team format, you must have some sort of strategy or pattern to play by. The right tactics will mean that you are constructively rationalising your game and making maximum use of your best weapons to exploit the vulnerable areas of your opponent's game.

Every game is different, so you must adopt different tactics accordingly. As we have already seen, some things are beyond your control — your opponent's luck, for example — but there are some general guidelines which apply to every game you play. Before we look at particular game situations where different stylists are pitted against one another, I propose to run through a number of general tips which might help you.

Every player has what we call an area of indecision. In simple terms, this is a stroke about which you have to make a split-second conscious decision as to whether to use your forehand or your backhand. Normally, if the ball comes straight to your forehand side then you will automatically use your forehand. But what if the ball comes down the middle straight into your playing shoulder? As you probably know, this is a much harder customer to deal with.

This area of indecision varies from one person to another and is governed by the position of the playing shoulder in relation to the rest of the table. In the course of a rally it will vary from shot to shot according to where your opponent's playing shoulder is at the time. To close the game down and contain it you should seek to exploit this area of play, particularly against a fast forehand-oriented looper.

Time finding out about your opponent is time well spent. Playing for my country makes this a lot easier for me than for many other people. Before

A moment of jubilation for Klampar on winning the 1980 European Top Twelve, in Hungary.

12. Winning tactics

a European League match we have a look at any video tapes we might have of my previous encounters with a particular player, and of any recent matches she may have played. You might not have access to sophisticated facilities like that, but talk about your opponents with fellow players — where are they weak, where are they strong? What services do they play, how do they respond to different services? Do they flick or push the short serve? How do they react to spin? Can they read spin? Are they one-pace players — would they collapse under a variation of pace?

These are the main areas that you should be looking at and familiarising yourself with. On many occasions, though, you do not get the chance to check out the opposition. Your first opportunity might only be on the table, face to face. Nevertheless, use the one- or two-minute knock-up before the game starts to your best possible advantage. For example, never show off your best services until play commences. As a defender, I never chop a ball during the knock-up. The reason for this is simple; I do not want the other player in any way to become fluent in playing the chopped ball. As a result they have to acclimatise themselves — at the risk of losing points — once the game has started.

Likewise, as a combination-bat player, I never hit the ball with the anti-loop side of my bat during the knock-up. Again, why let your opponent become unnecessarily familiar with the weapons at your disposal? They can inspect your bat as the rules permit (and you should always have a look at theirs) but they cannot force you to play with both sides of it during the knock-up.

The last thing before the game actually starts is the toss to decide who is to serve, or the choice of ends. Some people prefer to give the service away. The thinking behind this is usually that at 18−17 in the third they will be serving and will have the advantage. Personally, I think this is a bizarre way to approach the game. Not only is it negative, as you should be thinking in terms of winning in two straight, but it could get you off to a bad start in the first game by allowing the other player the advantage of the service. Unless there is a noticeable difference in the quality of ends (which is very rare these days) take the serve if you win the toss.

Another myth about serving which I have often come across is the notion of only using your best services toward the end of the game, when the scores are close. I have never been able to understand this piece of advice. My view is that if you have got some good services up your sleeve, use them. Make sure your opponent does not get used to them, though; but in a batch of five services those that he finds the most awkward to return can be used two or even three times. After all, you may not even get to 20-all if you don't use them!

Of course, tactics are not confined to the table itself. In team matches, playing order and a careful selection of the players available can contribute to the success of the team. For example, it is always useful to have a defender in your squad of players. In European League matches (which are the best of seven encounters) the team does not need to nominate until the match is practically under way.

Certain countries like Sweden and Czechoslovakia have players who can be vulnerable to combination-bat defenders. In this instance, Peter Simpson, the national trainer, will almost certainly include either Douggie Johnson or John Hilton in the men's part of the squad.

In local league matches, the order in which the games are played can sometimes be chosen alternately by the opposing captains. Exploit this system if it is the case in your local league, and use your best players to 'soften up' members of the opposition for when they come to play the weaker members of your side.

Playing against different styles

In table tennis today, there are basically three styles of player — the attacker, the defender and the blocker. It is not quite as clear-cut as this, but most players fall roughly into one of these three categories. There are few effective all-rounders about.

Depending on what type of player you are, here is my analysis of all the permutations involving these three stylists, and my tips for each.

Attacker versus attacker

When two attackers face each other, the key to the game is the quality of service and receive and getting in first with the topspin ball. The service has got to be tight so as to get the right sort of third ball back. When receiving, therefore, wherever possible you should try to make the return by flicking the ball deep into the server's playing shoulder.

Recent trends in the attacking game seem to have come from the Swedes who have taken to serving fast and long and then topspinning the already topspun return hard and straight off the bounce, which requires a carefully-judged bat angle to be effective.

When forced away from the table the attacker can occasionally be found wanting on the backhand wing. If you are an attacking player faced with an opponent of similar style to yourself, try and expose this area of your opponent's game early on. By testing in this way, you will quickly find out if he is weak there. If so, turn the screw and apply the pressure.

12. Winning tactics

Michael Appelgren of Sweden — the 1982 European Men's Singles winner at only 20 years old.

Attacker versus blocker

The key to the success of the blocker is to feed off the pace of the attacker. Let him topspin — but not well. The good blocking player will sometimes punch the ball hard, sometimes block it very soft, but will always try to get in off any loose balls. If you favour this sort of game, do not rely on your reflexes alone and just half-volley all the time — be prepared to attack as well. When you do, force the ball into the opponent's body with plenty of spin, or wide down the backhand.

In my opinion, the best blocker in the world is England's Desmond Douglas. In the vanguard of the all-time great topspinners is Dragutin Surbek of Yugoslavia. When they are drawn to play one another a memorable encounter usually takes place. If Douglas takes the bit between his teeth and goes at the ball he can make life very hard for Surbek and in this sort of situation I would back him to win. However, Surbek is always difficult to beat and the way he approaches a game with Douglas is to vary the pace, using plenty of spin to force the openings for his powerful forehand kill.

This is roughly how the attacker should deal with the half-volley player. Playing at one pace will only unduly familiarise your opponent, who will quickly lapse into a rhythm, developing a fluency which will be difficult to

Playing against different styles 139

overcome. Indeed, the players who play Desmond well are the likes of Gergely of Hungary and Appelgren of Sweden. They exploit the area of indecision particularly well and are quite vicious with the loose ball.

Defender versus attacker

The basis of my game, and that of a lot of players who are defenders like me, is to wear down attackers and force them to make errors.

I do this by mixing the chopped ball with the floated one, moving the ball around, usually deep into my opponent's half of the table, and attacking the third ball when possible. It is important that defensive players

Desmond Douglas, the fastest reflex player in the world.

12. Winning tactics

Liang Ke Liang of China — a 'third ball' specialist.

are capable of hitting when necessary. It means that your opponent can never comfortably develop a rhythm or afford to play anything less than perfectly, or you will put it neatly away.

To play this sort of game demands patience and concentration, which are exactly the two qualities that the attacker needs to overcome the defender. One of the best attacking players I ever saw against the chopper was former England player Trevor Taylor. His attitude was to 'reverse the boredom process', as he put it. If necessary, he would be prepared to topspin ten, twenty, even thirty balls to get the right sort of opening which would allow him to kill the ball. Because of his incredible tenacity, it was usually the defender who would become frustrated and start making the unforced errors.

When faced with a defender, be prepared to work hard and wait. Vary the pace using slow and fast topspin, dropshotting when the ball is short and following up with a fast one down the middle, all the time moving your opponent about. This is important, because a key part of the defensive game is to tempt you into making silly mistakes. Like Trevor Taylor, reverse this principle, and move the ball all over, putting as much pressure on your opponent to make the errors.

Playing against different styles

Pak Yung Sun of North Korea, World Champion in 1977 and 1979 — one of the best players in the world against the chopped ball.

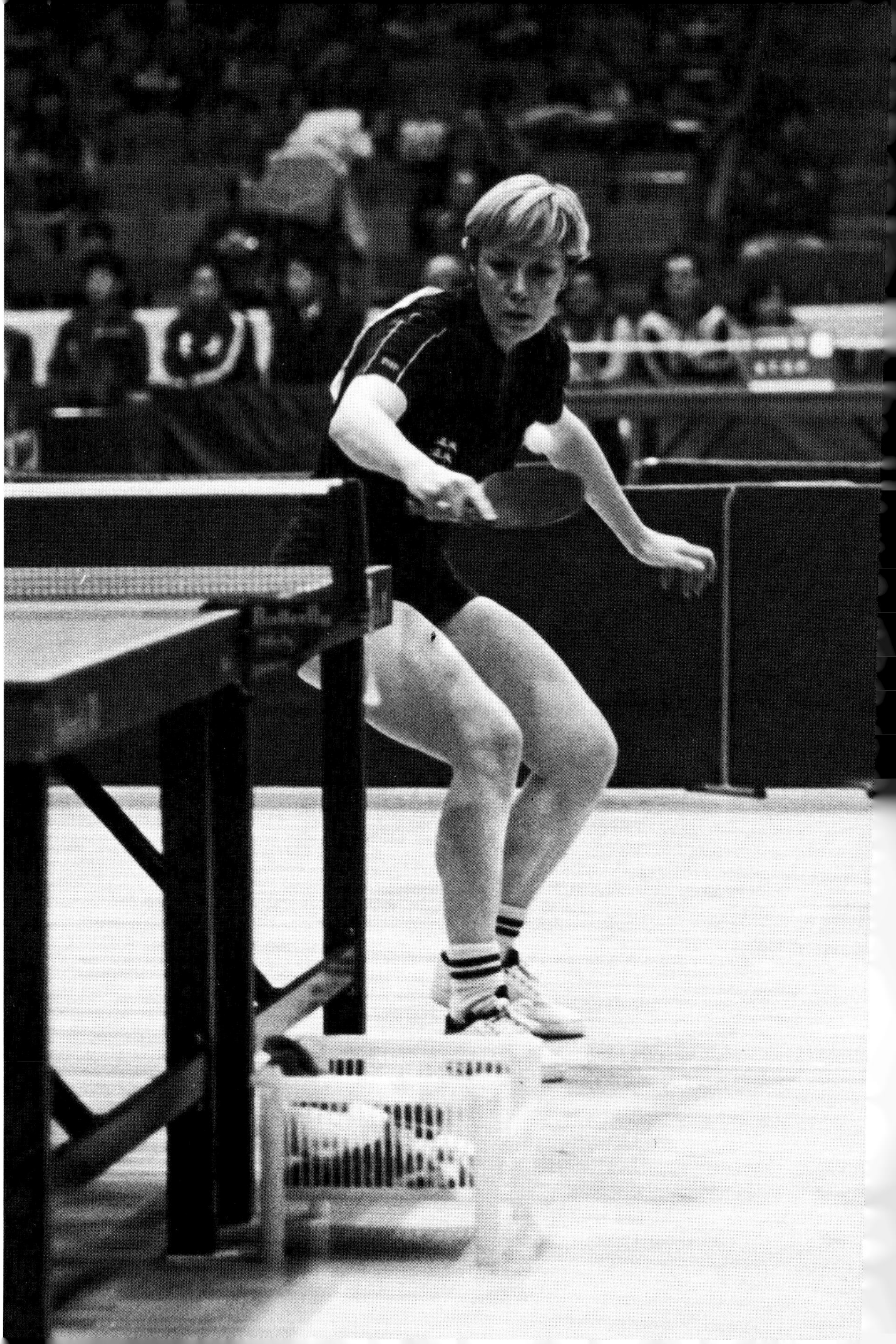

Defender versus blocker

A good defender will almost always fare well against the blocker. This is because many blockers do not have the power to break through a good chop defence. As a defender, then, you can afford to relax a little and not attack as many 50–50 balls. The tactics you adopt are roughly the same as for the attacker, varying spin and pace and waiting for the right one to kill.

The obligation is then on the blocker to adapt and not fall for the defender's usual tricks. One of the best illustrations I can give you occurred when I played Romania's Olga Nemes in the 1982 European Championships in Budapest. She is one of the rising young stars of Europe and was only sixteen at the time. The year before, in the World Championships, I had overcome her with little difficulty; then, she tried to topspin the ball past me but was simply not strong enough and I won in single figures.

This time, though, she had clearly learned that topspinning was not the way to win. Instead she pushed the ball a lot more, very tightly, long and short, and waited for me to play with the anti-loop side of my bat. Then she quickly moved round and flat-hit through the ball, very hard. I was taken by surprise, having been lulled into a false sense of security by our previous encounter. Though I eventually pulled through, this proved to be the hardest game I had before the final.

Defender versus defender

This is not the most exciting game for the spectator and for the two players it is more an exercise in determination. If the expedite rule is to be used, it is almost always in this situation. Quite simply, neither player wants to give anything away and neither has a strong enough attack to break through.

The rules have recently been amended so that, subject at the outset to the agreement of both players, the expedite rule can be played right from the first point. Personally, I never opt for this arrangement. I prefer to wait until the statutory fifteen minutes are up, when the expedite becomes law. This is because I prefer to win points in my own time and would rather be faced with an expedite game when the score is, say, 10–6 or so in my favour. I am then in the driving seat, and the pressure is more on my opponent to win the points.

There are few tactical tips I can give you for the defender versus defender game, except to be patient, be prepared to wait and play for a long time if need be. Whatever happens, do not lose your cool.

In the final of the 1976 European Championships at Prague in Czechoslovakia, I played Maria Alexandru of Romania. A defender like

The author showing good poise close to the table.

12. Winning tactics

Taken during the 1976 European Ladies' Singles Final, the author shuts her mind off as her opponent and the umpire disagree.

myself, she was, at the time, the more experienced player and fancied by everyone to win.

We inevitably got into the expedite situation where the obligation is on the server (both players serve alternately) to win the point in under twelve balls. An incident occurred in which someone got their counting wrong. I had served, and Maria was adamant that I had let thirteen balls go by before I killed the ball past her. The umpire and officials disagreed, saying I had killed the twelfth ball and as a result I had won the point.

A row developed between Maria and the umpires, which was the last thing I needed at that point. I had to keep my concentration and remain oblivious to what was going on. If I had let my thoughts wander, I would surely have paid the consequences when the game resumed. For fifteen minutes the dispute raged as I sat slumped on the floor shutting myself off from it. In retrospect, I am convinced that it was my determination and emotional and mental strength that carried me through and gave me the title. They were certainly the decisive factors on this occasion, but relate more to psychology than to outright tactics.

Blocker versus blocker

In this sort of encounter, the winner is the player who is thoughtful enough to keep his/her opponent guessing. I have talked to many players who have played Desmond Douglas and complain that he seems to know where the ball is going before it has even been hit. This is principally why he is such a brilliant exponent of this type of game.

It is important that you are flexible enough to adapt. Consider going away from the table a little and topspinning the ball up. Your opponent may be caught out, and could overreact by trying to force the ball too much, hopefully off the end of the table.

In simple terms, take the initiative and avoid playing to your opponent's strengths, which are obviously the wings. Use the middle of the table to force the loose half-volley which, if you are quick enough, you should be able to kill.

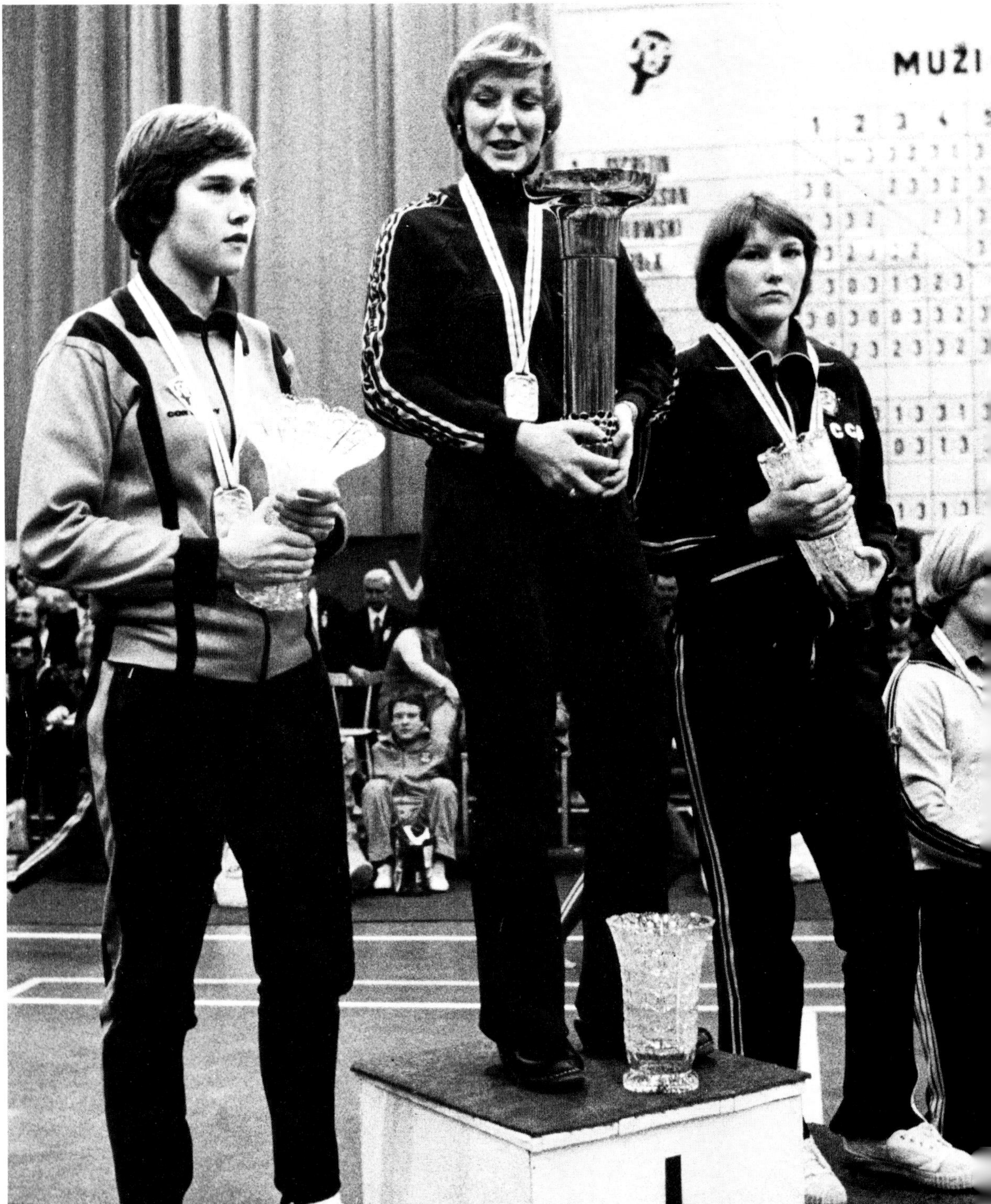
MUŽI

13 Training through the seasons

Periodisation

One of the most noticeable shortcomings of British sport is how we never seem to clinch the big one. There have been exceptions, of course, but there have been so many instances when we have failed at the last and most crucial hurdle. We produce runners who record the fastest times ever and tennis players who are capable of beating anyone. Yet our Olympic Gold Medallists and Wimbledon Champions are too few and far between.

Take for example Brendan Foster, the distance runner, or Sue Barker, the tennis player. The former never quite managed to beat Lasse Viren in an event like the Olympics or European Championships, yet could win convincingly in a less prestigious event. Sue Barker has shown herself capable of winning against many of the world's top players but at Wimbledon will often lose disappointingly to an opponent of much lesser standing.

Particularly in ball games, such as table tennis, it is not always the most skilful player who will win in a top-class event. I have seen many cases where a player of only moderate ability will overcome a far more gifted opponent. More often than not, the reason for this is quite simple. The former is playing to his full potential — peaking — while the latter is playing perhaps below average by his standards. Nevertheless, a below-average performance is usually the difference between winning and losing: it is not always the most gifted that will win, but the best prepared.

This is not to denigrate the value of skill in modern table tennis. Except at a very high level, it is without question an essential commodity and the most important factor governing a player's performance. It is a different story in athletics, however, where fitness and (depending on the event in question) technique are decisive.

Nevertheless, we have no shortage of skilful exponents in England who cannot deliver the goods at the right time. Indeed, it has been a major headache for English coaches to know how to nurture their players into peaking at the right time. At every World or European Championships there are perhaps a dozen or more people capable of taking the title, yet the

Winner of the gruelling European top twelve event in 1978, at Prague.

same ones appear on or near the winners' rostrum every year. Earlier in the year, though, those same players may be having disastrous results.

Jonyer of Hungary is a typical example. At the beginning of the season he is very up and down. Around November or December his results are average. But in spring — the time of the World or European Championships — it is a safe bet that he will be playing well.

You do not have to be a psychologist to see that these peak performances at the right time are not the sporadic, uncontrollable phenomena they at first sight appear. It is possible to realise them by careful preparation and planning using the right training programme. This notion of preparing a sportsman to give his best performance at a specified time is nothing new. It was developed by a Russian sports scientist named Matveyev, and the technique has since become known as 'periodisation'.

Professor Matveyev worked largely in track and field athletics. He closely examined the performances of several thousand top-class athletes in events where it is relatively easy to quantify the results — the fastest time, the furthest throw, the heaviest weight. He compared the results of the athletes over a period of time with an analysis of the intensity of training during the same period. His main discovery was that his subjects generally achieved one, or in some instances, only two peaks in a twelve-month period. With this in mind, he came up with a set of theories as to how one might be able to reach the peak performance at the appropriate time.

The training cycle

A carefully planned training cycle is set out which has three distinct elements to it; a preparatory period, a competitive period and a recuperative period. There should be no more than two such cycles in any one year, though these can be cycles such that two or more peaks occur at the end of each cycle. This is in cases where there is a high technical content involved, such as jumping or throwing, or indeed a game like table tennis.

The concept of dividing up the training year into specific periods has become common to most sports. However, since about the late 1960s, largely because of Matveyev's research, it has become far more sophisticated. Several Eastern European nations have embraced the technique completely and developed it specifically for table tennis.

They have gone so far as to adjust their domestic competitive calendars to provide for it. They have also arranged for their own international open tournaments to be held at a suitable interval from the World or European Championships which alternate every two years.

Dusan Osmanayic, who for many years coached the Yugoslavian team, compares the approach to the dilemma faced by the farmer. If he tries to grow the maximum crop each year from the same field he will inevitably lose all the nutrients from the soil. Subsequent harvests will then deteriorate, so he must make sure he rests the soil and rotates his crops instead.

So it is with a leading table-tennis player. Experience has shown that to divide the year into short periods of preparation only results in an incomplete mastery of technique, unstable performance and perhaps inadequate fitness.

Let us look at the three stages of the periodisation cycle and how they have been applied to table tennis, working on the basis of two peaks in each season.

Phase 1 — active rest

This first phase of the cycle ideally lasts between 2 and 2½ months in the first cycle, and less in the second. The main aim is to try to maintain stamina and endurance, but in a fashion far from arduous.

The Yugoslavians, for example, take the players to a team camp up in the mountains. They never pick up a table-tennis bat during the course of their stay. Hiking, jogging and generally relaxing are the order of the day, building up team spirit and dissipating the mental pressures of the preceding season.

Phase 2 — preparation

Having rested, the players go about the strenuous task of retrieving their optimum level of match fitness. This takes place over a period of around 2½ to 3 months.

The first two weeks or so are away from the table and are devoted to a concentrated programme of endurance training and improving the aerobic capacity or recovery rate. Because table tennis is the sort of game where short, sharp bursts of intense activity are not uncommon, it is essential that you can recover your resting state as quickly as possible. Short sprints within a long run is an exercise that helps to achieve this.

The nature of the physical training undertaken changes as the phase progresses. Naturally, flexibility and loosening exercises are done as a prelude to any intense physical session so as to avoid unnecessary injury. Any longer-distance cardiovascular work is done early on in the build-up. Any heavy weights, if used at all, occur early in the phase. As the competitive phase draws closer the resistances are decreased and the repetitions are increased. The sprint sessions should become more frequent as the phase progresses, but the distances should get shorter, with more repetitions.

Equally, the nature of the table practices changes as the competitive phase draws closer. At the beginning, they should be designed to improve on table fitness and consistency; for example, regular footwork exercises around the table. A few of the England squad like to use the training robot in this respect — it never gets bored as a human practice controller might. By firing balls continuously at specified intervals and at preset speeds it enables a player to 're-groove' his stroke play and iron out any problems with technique.

Towards the end of the phase the practices include more tactical content and take on a competitive nature, recreating as far as possible a matchplay situation. Players are trying to win points using specific tactical ploys and concentrating on touch and table skills.

Phase 3 — competition

By now, physical exercise is minimal and just enough to maintain the status quo. Gentle jogging should be used along with the usual flexibility exercises on the morning of the event.

At an event like the World or European Championships many of the players will practise for the hour preceding their first match. Obviously, the practices are specific to the style of the opponent to be played, but generally they follow a similar pattern: establishing a consistency, followed by service and receive routines.

The difference between winning and losing can be so slight at this level that it is essential that the player's touch is just right.

The diagram shows the competitive table-tennis year and how the periodised year is built around it.

Because of the marginal nature of high-level table tennis, coaches are forced to be open-minded about the value of any fresh approach such as periodisation. No doubt you will be keen to know whether it would be of any value to a strong local league or county player.

I am afraid that I cannot tell you, because I have no information as to whether or not it has been tried at this level. There are practical problems with implementing it here but there are similar difficulties at a national level as well which I will discuss shortly. However, this should not preclude any such player from having a go.

Using the diagram, first identify two occasions when you consider it important that you do well. They might be the town team or county trials at the beginning of the season, and the town championships in the spring. Hopefully they will be separated by about five or six months.

The training cycle   151

The periodised table-tennis year.

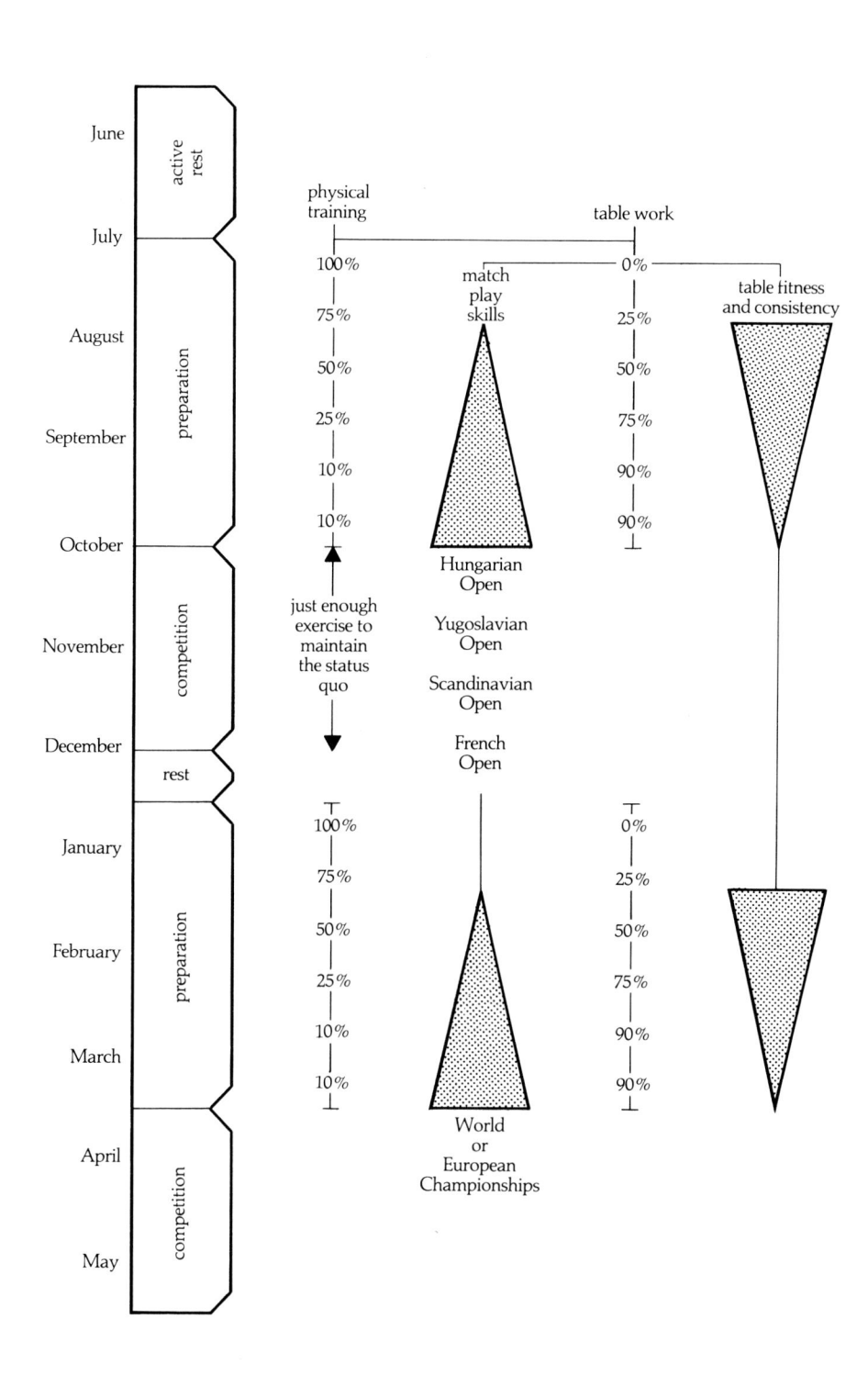

June	active rest
July	
August	preparation
September	
October	
November	competition
December	rest
January	preparation
February	
March	
April	competition
May	

physical training — **table work**

100% — 0% — table fitness and consistency
75% — 25%
50% — match play skills — 50%
25% — 75%
10% — 90%
10% — 90%

Hungarian Open
Yugoslavian Open
Scandinavian Open
French Open

just enough exercise to maintain the status quo

100% — 0%
75% — 25%
50% — 50%
25% — 75%
10% — 90%
10% — 90%

World or European Championships

13. Training through the seasons

Then build up your preparatory phases around these two peaks. Remember to shift your practices gradually: from regular to irregular footwork, from set directional pieces to random ball switches, from one-pace practices to multi-pace; develop a consistency in topspin or chop before cultivating a variation in speed of spin.

Above all, though, ensure that you take at least one period of 'active rest', preferably at the end of the season during the early summer months. As I said before, active rest means no table tennis.

The general types of exercise that a player should practise as he progresses through the preparation phase. They are examples only, and should be varied according to the player's style. In each case the targets can be changed.

First quarter of preparation phase:
Emphasis on 'grooving in' techniques and developing consistency. All exercises are down one line of play.

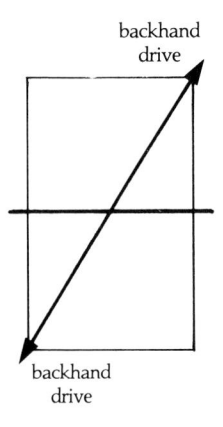

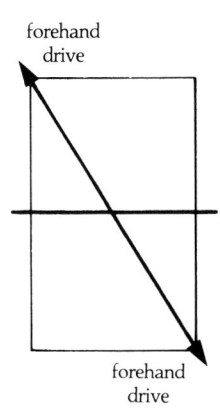

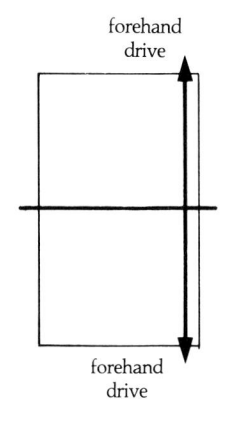

Second quarter of preparation phase:
Emphasis on 'grooving in' correct footwork patterns. All exercises are played to a set pattern.

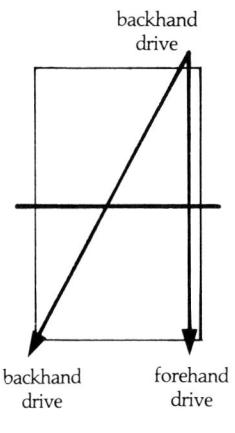

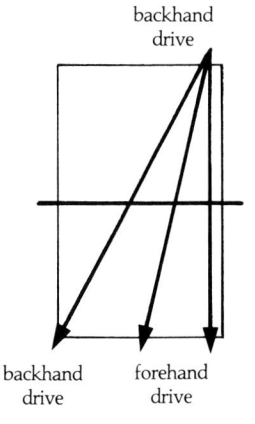

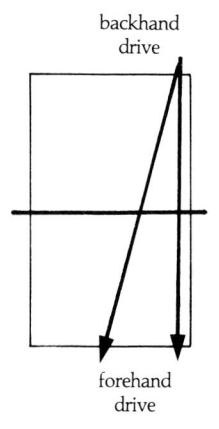

Does it work?

Naturally, you cannot conclusively prove that the periodised method of training is successful. For that matter, it is almost impossible to prove that any method of training will automatically bring about good results.

There are so many factors other than just good preparation which bring about a good performance — or, more often, a bad one. Late flights, an uncomfortable night's sleep, a row with a journalist or a difficult official, or just plain bad luck. All these are circumstances that you simply cannot foresee, but they could totally unbalance you at the worst possible time.

However, it is difficult to ignore the fact that the World or European Championships are nearly always six months or so after the Hungarian, French, Yugoslavian and Scandinavian Open Championships. Clearly the coaches in these countries are adopting a systematic approach to the training year. A quick glance at the list of winners in the past few years of the European Men's Singles and Doubles Events gives a most interesting impression.

Third quarter of preparation phase:
Emphasis on speeding up footwork and improving anticipation. Random play, with players now playing strokes they would use in a match.

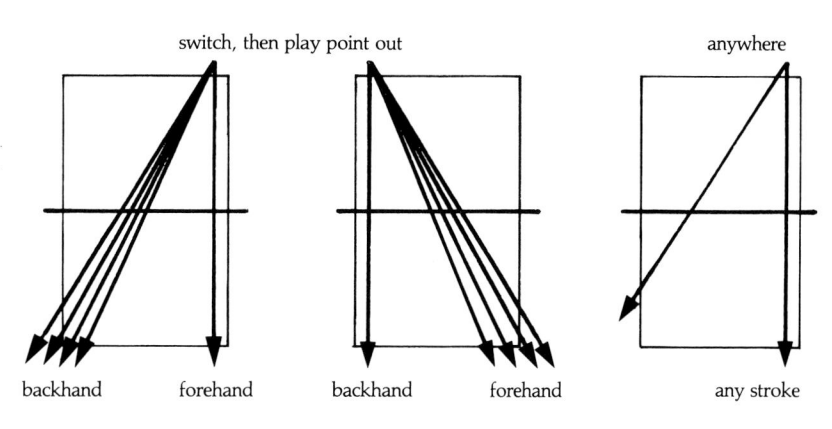

switch, then play point out

anywhere

backhand   forehand   backhand   forehand   any stroke

Final quarter of preparation phase:
Emphasis on improving service and receive ready for the competitive phase. Match-play exercises with a lot of free play.

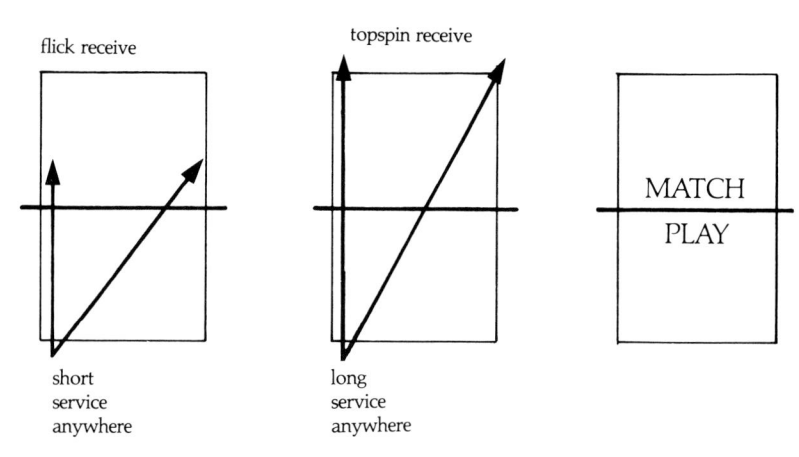

flick receive

topspin receive

MATCH PLAY

short service anywhere

long service anywhere

13. Training through the seasons

Year	Singles	Doubles
71/72	Bengtsson (Sweden)	Jonyer + Rosas (Hungary)
73/74	Orlowski (Czechoslovakia)	Jonyer + Klampar (Hungary)
75/76	Secretin (France)	Bengtsson + Johansson (Sweden)
77/78	Gergely (Hungary)	Gergely + Orlowski (Hungary + Czechoslovakia)
79/80	Hilton (England)	Secretin + Birocheau (France)
81/82	Applegren (Sweden)	Surbek + Kalinic (Yugoslavia)

Since about 1976, England has tried to adopt this approach. Three training camps are held for the World or European Championships at carefully-planned intervals to fit in with the concept of a double-periodised year. From a personal point of view, the years since have been the most successful of my career. Here are the details of my performances in the European Championships since 1976.

Year	Venue	Team Event Results	Individual Events Results
1976	Prague	Won 9 out of 11	Women's Singles Champion Women's Doubles Champion
1978	Duisberg	Won 7 out of 10	Women's Singles Runner-up
1980	Berne	Won 10 out of 10	Lost in last 16 of singles
1982	Budapest	Won 13 out of 13	Women's Singles Runner-up

With the exception of John Hilton's victory in 1980, my other English colleagues have not enjoyed the same success. There may be a variety of reasons for this but I am sure that one is because most of them have to spend a lot of their time on the English tournament circuit. Without doubt a number of them are talented enough to succeed in the international arena. They have to compete in domestic tournaments to maintain their ranking and as a result their place in the squad. Many have to compete to earn a living or to satisfy their commitments to equipment sponsors. There are times when they must play, though they would get more benefit from a good rest; and continually there are up-and-coming junior players snapping at their heels.

Nevertheless, given this situation, it is impossible for them to immerse themselves in the careful timing and training of a double-periodised year.

Fortunately, I have had some immunity from these pressures, and I have managed to keep hold of a high England ranking with comparative ease, for the last few years. My selection for England has become almost automatic, owing to my success abroad. This leaves me the breathing space in which to be able to train when I want to, and to choose not to play, in accordance with the programme.

Desmond Douglas has been one of England's most consistently successful players since he left the junior ranks in the mid-1970s. For a number of years now he too has had little difficulty maintaining his national number-one ranking. His playing commitments are wide and varied, playing for England in European League Fixtures, in overseas tournaments, in Top Twelve and Masters Grand Prix events around the world. He also plays in the financially lucrative German Bundesliga: in table-tennis terms, at least, he is one of the top money earners in the game. In my opinion he works extremely hard for every penny he gets.

Yet despite Desmond's European League and Bundesliga results being second to none, he has yet to finish in the reckoning for a World or European title. I am convinced that this is purely because he is playing too much because of his extensive competitive commitments. He is unable to approach the season with any form of planned preparation in mind. Even though he gives a uniformly high level of performance throughout the season, he is never at an absolute peak at the end when it counts most.

To be in with a good chance at the World or European Championships you cannot afford to be playing at anything less than at your best. People peak to different extents. I have already mentioned the case of Jonyer. The difference between his playing poorly and playing well is probably somewhere in the region of fifteen points. Desmond, on the other hand, varies by only about three points but those three points can be decisive in the final analysis.

It would be quite wrong of me to suggest that this approach is the elusive factor that produces champions. One of the difficulties I have found with a periodised approach is how to assess your level of performance. If you happen to be able to win fairly comfortably within your own country it is impossible to measure how well you are playing without competing abroad. But the programme is specific in its avoidance of the strain of hard competition at the wrong time.

To do well in the World Championships it goes without saying that you have to be at a mental peak as well. To have a successful team event you are playing for five days with two matches each day. There is a day's rest, and then the individual events start. To do well in these too, you have to sustain this strength of character, even though psychologically you have a natural tendency to relax once the pressure of the team event is over. There are many instances of players who have excelled in the team event but have failed to extend their resolve to the individual events, and so end up disappointed.

13. Training through the seasons

If periodisation is going to have any chance of success it needs the backing of everyone involved in the game. At the moment, the top English players have too many conflicting loyalties, and the pressures they face come from all directions: their local league with whom they started, possibly their county side, tournament organisers, their national league side, their sponsor. All these people are relying heavily on the player, who in turn understands the need to put something back in when the occasion demands it.

The English Table Tennis Association has made some advances, though: the domestic tournament calendar has now been planned to take account of foreign events. I hope this is only the start, and that in years to come the facilities will become available to allow the talent in England to gain the success it so richly deserves.

England's Karen Witt, a gifted young player with all the qualities to make the top.

Desmond Douglas — supremely talented, but will he ever be a World Champion?

14 The Chinese scene

A book on table tennis would be incomplete without some mention of the Chinese. Indeed, whenever it crops up in conversation that I am a table-tennis player, particularly when I meet new people, the same question always seems to crop up: 'Why are the Chinese so good at that game?' China, and table tennis, it would seem, go hand in hand with one another.

Whenever the Chinese team tours this country, the sport arouses the interest of the media as never before. Tickets sell out overnight, and the intelligentsia of table tennis fall over one another grasping at clues and searching for hidden meanings with a bearing on how they might perfect their own game.

It is not only the table-tennis fraternity that regards China with curiosity. The skill and adroitness they bring to any sport is magical, almost spiritual. Considering that China is the largest nation on earth — about one in four of the human race is of Chinese extraction — we still know relatively little about it in the West. I challenge you to name five Chinese cities; most people can get as far as Shanghai, Peking and Canton — but beyond that?

Our ignorance of this great nation must of course result partly from the fact that China deliberately isolated itself from the West, following Mao Tse-Tung's rise to power in 1949 and China's total adoption of his communist teachings. This isolation was compounded by his purging of the country through the cultural revolution during the later 1960s.

Naturally, this was reflected in their participation in world table-tennis affairs. As late as 1965, people like former world number-one Chuang Tse-Tung were thrilling British audiences. But for the next six years or so they completely disappeared from everything, including such prestigious events as the World Championships.

But it was through the World Championships of 1971 that the Chinese leadership chose to re-establish contact, not only with the world of table tennis, but with the political world. 'Pingpong diplomacy', the newspapers called it, and table tennis was used as the vehicle to re-establish diplomatic ties with Britain, the United States and may other nations.

1981 World Champion Guo Yue Hua of China.

The Chinese scene

When I left Heathrow Airport as part of the England Squad for those Championships, held in Nagoya, Japan, I had no idea what was to be in store for me. Out of the blue, toward the end of the event, we received an invitation from the People's Republic of China to tour their country, play table tennis and make friends. The American squad received a similar invitation. Though as a rather innocent nineteen-year-old I did not realise the implications of it, I was to be one of a mere handful of Westerners who were permitted to enter their country during a period of well over five years. It was a trip I shall always remember with great fondness.

The author with her guide making the epic train journey from Hong Kong to Canton at the start of England's 1971 tour of the People's Republic.

The England party being met in the early hours of the morning at Peking by the Chinese team.

It was the first of a number of tours that English teams were to make. In 1973, my husband and co-author Don Parker was part of an England Junior Squad that made the same epic journey. Like myself in 1971 he was given a warm and cordial reception that permeated down from senior politicians to local rice pickers. For a country that has embraced the collectivist lifestyle so completely, I have never come across so many individuals and compulsively entertaining eccentrics.

In spite of the fact that they had not competed outside their own country for over five years, their players were still streets ahead of us. This would not have been immediately apparent to any impartial observer, though. Because our visit was so steeped in political overtones, their players had been primed to 'go easy'. As a result we found we were winning more points than we were truly capable of. The Chinese toured Britain shortly after and occasionally we even beat them. Nevertheless we all knew that any successes owed more to politics and 'friendship matches' than to any superior ability we might have had.

To the Chinese, though, this approach was based purely in a desire to be friendly. Unfortunately, by some of our players it was seen as patronising and insulting. Nowadays, the Chinese understand that true friendship in sport comes out of spirited competition. The tour they made of Britain in early 1982 saw them annihilate all opposition with a very young team that had hitherto not set foot outside their country.

To try to explain why they are so good at this game is far from easy. I can only conclude that it must have a lot to do with the fact that their society and culture is so radically opposite to that of Western nations.

The reason why table tennis is so popular there, springs from Mao's teachings. In a country that still has great difficulty feeding its enormous population, Mao instructed that all land-based sports should be rejected. They waste valuable areas that could be turned over to the production of food. Table tennis requires far less room, and, of course, can be played indoors. So Mao decreed that this was the type of sport the people should pursue.

The English party pictured with Chinese father-figure Chou En-Lai.

The author shaking hands with Premier Chou En-Lai.

The author and team-mate Pauline Piddock knock up in front of Peking factory workers.

It is also worth pointing out that they are not allowed to marry until they are twenty-five, and courting is actively discouraged among young people. The reason for this is that much of China's economy relies on labour-intensive industries. A young male will give his best physical work between eighteen and twenty-five, and the influence of the opposite sex will only distract him from his work in the community. Sport, such as table tennis, helps him burn off surplus energy, however, so it is encouraged among young people. And if his career happens to be as a full-time table-tennis player he will be able to devote himself to it wholly, without the distracting influence of young women. In any event, it seems to work. Few Chinese men marry before their late twenties or early thirties.

Though recent reports indicate that they are allowing more Western influences in, they still largely reject our materialistic way of life. A couple of instances spring to mind which illustrate this.

14. The Chinese scene

At the Great Wall of China.

The English team with thousands of Chinese onlookers stroll across the People's Square in Peking.

An old Chinese lady with her feet bound tightly in lengths of cloth since early childhood. This is a legacy that stretches back to pre-revolutionary days.

14. The Chinese scene

Alan Hydes, a member of the England squad on that spontaneous 1971 tour, lost a button off his jacket while shopping in one of their stores. He had barely noticed this on returning to the team's hotel when a couple of boiler-suited Chinese who had found it arrived to return the button to its owner. Some of the team once left a tip at their hotel by way of thanks for the friendly, efficient service. As they were about to board the plane at the airport twenty miles away, a member of the hotel staff sprinted across the tarmac to hand it back to them. He had presumed that they had either lost or forgotten their money. The notion of tipping was completely alien to them, implying, as it does, some sort of élitism.

They are a people of impeccable manners. We once went swimming at the local public baths, and before we got near the water they completely vacated the pool. This was not because of pressure from any nearby party official, but a totally spontaneous reaction on the part of the swimmers themselves. When I questioned them through our interpreter, the reply was that we were their guests, and surely would we not enjoy our swim better with no one else in the pool? At a later dinner held in our honour I confessed to a liking for cream cakes, only to be bombarded at subsequent meals (breakfast included) with platefuls of them!

Both teams pictured in the People's Stadium, Peking, prior to their friendship match.

This genial nature of humility and egalitarianism features strongly in their approach to table tennis. There is no such thing as hero worship; not once did I see anyone asking for the autograph of any of their leading players. This is particularly striking because table tennis is their number-one sport in much the same way as soccer is in Britain. In Peking there are at least three covered stadiums the size of the Wembley Empire Pool, and many more 'cultural halls' similar to our leisure centres. Our series of friendly matches attracted crowds of fifteen to twenty thousand identically dressed Chinese (presumably with their bicycles parked outside).

The day before the match we would practise with the same players we were due to play. This is again part of their philosophy, the attitude being that 'we play together so that we both might improve'. If the ball went out of play it would travel for yards in the vastness of the arena. Instead of chasing after it we simply picked another ball from a nearby bucket, and young Chinese boys and girls would retrieve the stray ones. When we rested, the youngsters practised. I later learned that all their champions and national players have been ball boys at some time early in their careers.

Table tennis, being the national sport, is taught in the schools from a very young age, except that for the first year their youngsters are not allowed near a table, all they do is shadow play. When I talked to their coaches about this technique, they were quick to emphasise the importance of shadow play, not only at such a young age but even at national level, as an integral part of their training programme.

Because we have such an opposite, arguably less idealistic, culture we cannot honestly expect our sportsmen and sportswomen to display the same qualities of application and humility. Where our society encourages individual success and elitism, the emphasis in China is on teamwork; the individual is valued as a part of the whole.

They understand the need to be fit in quite different terms from ourselves. In the West, we are gradually becoming socially aware of the value of physical fitness, yet the Chinese have adopted it as a matter of priority and government policy. Each morning I saw the entire local community, irrespective of age, run through a brief warm-up routine. The reason for this is simple: a fit workforce is an efficient workforce. Days off work through sprained muscles reduce this efficiency. Each person understands and, more significantly, appreciates this principle, that their most important role is to work for the people, not themselves.

This of course extends to table tennis. Their gifted but less psychologically well equipped players will be part of the national squad, even though they might not be winners like their colleagues.

When the Hungarians took the World Team Title in Calcutta in 1977, the Chinese monopoly on the game was dramatically broken for a short while.

14. The Chinese scene

A crowd of over 25,000 witnesses the first foreign competition in their country for over five years.

This title means more to them than any other, because it is essentially the nation that is winning the trophy. This philosophy cannot be as readily reconciled with success in an individual event, and significantly the Chinese are not as successful in this area. The players are doing a job and are merely part of a squad including the coach, the lady who irons the kit, the children who collect the balls and so forth.

So as not to be caught out again by the Hungarians' powerful topspin game, one of the Chinese players of lesser temperament was instructed to learn to play exactly like Istvan Jonyer, and another like Tibor Klampar. The purpose of this was to allow their colleagues in the team to become totally familiar with that particular style of play. The players in question would have no qualms about this and everyone would automatically understand that they were fulfilling as important a role as any member of the national team.

It is not purely because of cultural differences that the Chinese are so much better. There are other reasons. Their coaches are particularly well qualified and trained, working full-time. Their basic needs in life — food, accommodation and money — are all found by the state. Equipment and training facilities are similarly provided for.

The combined effect of this extraordinary and quite singular approach to table tennis is that they are the best players in the world. No other nation places as much importance on the game, or devotes as many resources to it.

As a result their perfect technique in the vital areas of service and receive is second to none. Where we are less inclined to devote as much energy to what makes for boring practice, they are the opposite. Because of the attention they pay to service, they are invariably the innovators of new service techniques. Hsu Hsu-Fao, now non-playing captain of Italy, was dazzling opponents with the high-toss service back in 1973. Only in recent years has it become a feature of the European game.

Their technique is so well 'grooved in' that at, say, 19—20 down in the fifth and final game of the World Championships, they will show no hesitation in going for the 50—50 ball. Their humility and respect for their opponents means that you very rarely see any displays of temperament.

Students of the game that I talk to often mistakenly identify other factors, such as their bats, as being one of the key factors in the Chinese success. There is absolutely no mystery about Chinese bats. They are very happy to let you inspect them, even knock up with them. They are usually very tatty, and the rubber, if anything, is not as good a quality as ours. The only noticeable difference from our equipment is that instead of regularly replacing the combined rubber and sponge unit as we do, they choose to leave the sponge element and only replace the rubber part, which is made from natural rubber as opposed to the synthetic rubber marketed in the West.

While they can impart incredible spin, they seem to place more emphasis on deception — the ball that looks as though it is loaded with spin but is completely dead. They also seem to flat-hit the ball a lot, rather than topspin it.

It is true that they have exploited the use of the combination bat extremely well, and perhaps, as I have argued elsewhere, to the detriment of the game as a spectator sport. Whether the laws relating to this type of bat will change, very much depends on the attitude of the Chinese. A move against the combination bat is clearly not in their interests. With Chinese coaches in many of the developing table-tennis countries, it will be interesting to see if they sway the vote on this issue.

Even if the laws are changed, I do not think the Chinese domination of the game will be broken in the foreseeable future. They will adapt and concentrate on the task of working within whatever restrictions the authorities of the game dictate.

In the West we will still be bickering among ourselves, while the Chinese will be laying new foundations; they will remain, as ever, the true innovators in the world of table tennis.

15 What now for table tennis?

Table tennis is what P.E. teachers call a minority sport. I must concede that it is difficult to disagree with this view. But how do we elevate it above this meagre status, to the point where it will become recognised as a majority sport?

This has been a question which has been in the forefront of the minds of the English Table Tennis Association for a number of years now. It is not an issue that the players ignore, either. There is little money to be earned playing this game, when you consider the wage-packets of some of our counterparts in other racket sports. Indeed, if there were more money available, more talented players would emerge and we would be getting better results in the international arena.

Perhaps the first step in revitalising the game is the need to get more players, particularly at grass-roots level. Therefore, we must widen our net to catch more fish, and the obvious source of talent is in the school classrooms. We have an excellent schools' association pushing the game and running a hotly contested annual competition. This in itself, though, does not necessarily mean that more children are playing table tennis.

The only way to ensure this is for table tennis to be introduced as an established part of their physical education programme. For it to be a successful part of that physical education programme, the game must in turn become part of the established curriculum within colleges of physical education. In other words, teach the teachers.

In physiological terms the game sells itself to the educationalist. It can be a compulsive game to play and it will extend those children gifted with higher levels of skill. It is a particularly accessible game for women, and — contrary to popular opinion — can be organised quite easily to accommodate numbers that would be impossible in other racket sports. After all, you can get five tables onto an area the size of a badminton court, and with four per table that means twenty children gainfully occupied.

Wishful, but nonetheless realistic, thinking. Greater things, though, have been achieved in schools abroad, and not necessarily only in the communist-bloc countries. For example, Sweden, for years a pioneering

15. What now for table tennis?

table-tennis nation, has specialist schools in which children can develop their table tennis and receive their education at the same time. Erik Lindh, one of their latest batch of rising young stars, is a product of one such school at Falkenburg. Table-tennis schools, if you like, in the same way as Britain has independent schools that cater exclusively for talented young musicians. It seems only logical that exceptionally talented individuals should be found the facilities in which they can fully exploit their potential.

A rejuvenation of the game does not stop purely at getting table-tennis bats into more young hands than at present. As I have said elsewhere in this book, to succeed as a sport we must make table tennis an attractive and appealing game to play. We must entice the spectator back to our stadiums and tournaments.

But rallies only seem to last for three or four seconds. Strange bats make accomplished artists look like out-and-out novices. Suspect services get the thumbs down from English officials but approval in other countries. Various makes of table give quite different bounces and responses to spin. Balls, authenticated with international approval, show anything but a uniform quality between manufacturers. At the moment, the players, let alone the spectators, have enough difficulty in making out what is going on. The game, it would seem, is crying out for an element of standardisation in its equipment. Skill must be allowed to assert itself once more as the number-one factor in deciding between winner and loser.

It is not only a standardisation of equipment that is needed. The whole domestic tournament circuit needs revamping. At the moment spectator and player facilities leave much to be desired. Changing rooms and showers are a bonus, as is proper spectator seating, when both should really be a prerequisite. It is not unusual for players to be left completely in the dark about when they are likely to be called to the table, and spectators often miss the best matches because they do not know where or when they are due to take place. A stricter standardisation is called for, so that these events take on a professional look — which in turn will demand a more professional approach from the participants. Perhaps this will go towards cutting out the more questionable behaviour of some of our younger performers.

It might be worth reconsidering our scoring structure. Under the present 21-up system, the first 10 to 15 points are predominantly foundations upon which the final stages of the game are built. The crowd only gets involved at 13- or 14-all. Why not play more games, but only of 11-up, similar in a way to tennis? After only 5 or 6 points the spectators become interested, because by then the game is well under way. Then, perhaps, there will be some youngster watching, enthralled by the excitement, who will hang up his football boots and pester Father Christmas for a ping-pong bat.

Sweden's Erik Lindh — a product of the Falkenburg School of Table Tennis.

Despite my criticisms, there are developments in the game which are encouraging and which need to be capitalised on. The introduction of a National League is bringing about this much-needed professionalism among the English players. A number of national squad members now receive an annual retainer from the ETTA, which helps considerably in meeting their playing expenses. There are clubs such as Ellenborough, for example, which are purpose-built for table tennis. Open at all hours for players to practise, with showers, a bar and other social facilities — these all contribute to an increased enjoyment of the game, for both player and spectator.

It would be such a boost if we could have a national residential centre, where top players can live and practise, twenty-four hours a day if need be, with a couple of full-time top-class coaches on hand. To compete effectively overseas you need consistently good practice. Periodic training camps help, but are not enough to meet this demand fully.

From whatever angle we approach this question of the future of the game, we are inevitably drawn at some point to look at the governing bodies involved in its administration and, ultimately, its development. Concern for the game's prosperity should not lie exclusively with our national association, though. It percolates downward through regional and county associations to the local league, and in the long run, perhaps, these are the most important levels.

The picture I have gained of officialdom at all levels is one of hard-working, devoted people who do a thankless job. But while their dedication is never in doubt, their efforts are frequently misguided. Local league officials are parochial in their outlook, and to them table tennis is often no more than parlour ping-pong played in works canteens. Leisure centres are being built around them, but many seem unaware of the potential of these places for advertising their sport. National officialdom often displays a strange sense of priority. Archaic rules regarding dress are upheld vehemently by people who are running the game in their spare time.

Surely, the age of the spare-time volunteer, particularly in the highest echelons of our national association, is over. We need paid officials, perhaps even a chief executive and a team of corporate managers. We have shown remarkable foresight in choosing long ago to become an 'open' sport, and abolishing sham amateurism among the players, but we need to extend financial rewards to our elected officials as well. This would be a step in the right direction, making them more accountable, efficient — and above all, professional. There is absolutely no reason why this should not be introduced at the local level as well; many leagues would benefit from the addition of a paid organiser.

Underpinning all my arguments so far has been the implicit need for a substantial injection of cash. The limited resources of government agencies fall well short of what is truly required. But if darts and snooker can attract wealthy sponsors and such a lot of television exposure, why not table tennis? However, I feel sponsors will only be attracted if everyone connected with the game takes the initiative and works toward making some inroads into the areas I have outlined.

I hope that what I have said in this chapter will not put off any newcomers from taking up this splendid game. When all is said and done, we play for enjoyment, not prestige or material gain — and not necessarily even to win. I have had some great times in my career, and have seen a lot of the world, which would not have been possible without table tennis. You might not become a world-beater — but you will certainly have fun trying.

Good luck!